SPIRITUAL
TECHNOLOGY

Thank you for supporting independent publishing and the Systemology Society.

mardukite.com

MARDUKITE ACADEMY OF SYSTEMOLOGY COLLECTOR'S EDITION

SPIRITUAL TECHNOLOGY

A PRACTICAL GUIDE TO NEW STANDARD SYSTEMOLOGY (FOR SOLO-PILOTS & CO-PILOTS)

Advanced Training Supplement Manuals presented by Joshua Free

© 2025, JOSHUA FREE

ISBN : 978-1-961509-63-4

All Rights Reserved. No part of this publication may be reproduced in any form or by any means, electronic or mechanical, including photocopying, recording, artificial intelligence databases or systems, without permission from the publisher. This book is a religious artifact. It is not intended to diagnose any illness or substitute any medical treatment or professional health advice.

A MARDUKITE SYSTEMOLOGY PUBLICATION
Mardukite Research Library Catalogue No. "A.T.S."
Developed for Mardukite Academy & The Systemology Society
cum superiorum privilegio veniaque

FIRST EDITION
March 2025

Published from
Joshua Free Imprint – JFI Publications
Mardukite Borsippa HQ, San Luis Valley, Colorado

=== REACH HIGHER ===
Take Systemology to the Next Level!

This manual is a valuable companion for all Seekers applying New Standard Systemology techniques from the "Pathway to Ascension" Professional Course and the "Keys to the Kingdom" Advanced Training Course.

"Spiritual Technology" concisely organizes the most critical information necessary to expertly Solo-Pilot and Co-Pilot this applied philosophy.

It contains the original training supplements for the Mardukite Academy of Systemology (based on actual lectures given by Joshua Free) including: "Systemology Piloting," "Systemology Procedures" and "Systemology Biofeedback" (combined together with additional reference material from "Fundamentals of Systemology") in one portable collector's edition hardcover.

Discover how electronic devices measuring biofeedback were used to develop the "Pathway" and how they can enhance the effectiveness of your own personal progress. Defragment hidden areas of energetic turbulence, and free yourself from "spiritual implants" that have kept us all bound to the Matrix of this Physical Universe.

Never before has Joshua Free so effectively demonstrated the theory and practice of this spiritual technology — the "hows" and "whys" of these methods — clearly laid out for all Seekers to understand and use for themselves.

*Containing the original training supplements
for the Mardukite Academy of Systemology
Pathway to Ascension (professional course) and
Keys to the Kingdom (advanced training course)
all in one Collector's Edition Hardcover.*

MARDUKITE SYSTEMOLOGY SOCIETY "SPIRITUAL TECHNOLOGY" ADVANCED TRAINING SUPPLEMENTS

- Introducing New Standard Systemology ... 13
- A New View of the Human Spirit ... 14
- Charting Flights on the Pathway ... 16
- Taking Flight on the Pathway ... 17
- Your Future and Systemology ... 19

....
:: INTRODUCTING SYSTEMOLOGY PROCESSING ::
- Practices of Spiritual Awakening ... 23
- Basic Methods of Processing ... 24
- Systematic Processing Sessions ... 26
- Handling Presence In-Session ... 29
- The Formal Session ... 33

....
:: SYSTEMOLOGY PILOTING MANUAL ::
- Systematic Processing ... 41
- Preventative Fundamentals ... 42
- Traditional Piloting ... 44
- Elements of Piloting ... 47
- Piloting Seekers ... 50
- Entry-Points to a Session ... 52
- The Preliminary Interview ... 53
- The Skills of Piloting ... 56

....
:: SYSTEMOLOGY PROCEDURES MANUAL ::
- Systematic Processing and the Alpha-Spirit ... 65
- Systematic Procedures ... 68

- Preventative Fundamentals ... 76
- Psychosomatics and Pain ... 78
- Spiritual Implants and Entities ... 81
- Solo-Piloting Upper-Levels ... 85

....
:: SYSTEMOLOGY BIOFEEDBACK MANUAL ::
- Systemology and GSR-Biofeedback ... 91
- The History and Development
    of GSR-Biofeedback Metering ... 94
- Understanding GSR-Biofeedback
    for Spiritual Defragmentation ... 101
- Understanding GSR-Meters
    and Knowing How To Read Them ... 106
- Reading GSR-Biofeedback Meters ... 110
- Applying GSR-Meters
    to Systematic Processing ... 114
- Advanced Applications
    and the Professional Course ... 120

.... APPENDIX ....
- Foundations of Systemology ... 125
- The Standard Model of Systemology ... 129
- The Spheres of Existence ... 130
- Basic Systemology Glossary ... 131
- Additional Resources ... 152

∞

EDITOR'S NOTE

*"The Self does not actualize Awareness
past a point not understood."*
—*Tablets of Destiny*

This book is a companion to *New Standard Systemology*.
It contains supplemental materials for *Seekers* using
"The Pathway to Ascension" Professional Course and
the "Keys to the Kingdom" Advanced Training Course.
It is *not* a substitute for those course lessons.

A clear understanding of this material is critical for
achieving actual realizations and personal benefit
from applying our philosophy as spiritual technology.

If at any time you run across an unfamiliar term,
refer to the "Systemology Glossary" in the appendix
or a separate (complete) "Systemology Dictionary."
It is also helpful to keep a standard dictionary nearby.

The *Seeker* should not to simply "read through" this
book without also studying the related course lessons
and attaining proper comprehension as "knowledge."
Even when the information continues to be
"interesting"—if at any point you find yourself feeling
lost or confused while reading, trace your steps back.
Return to the point of misunderstanding
and go through it again.

Take nothing within this book on faith.
Apply the information directly to your life.

Decide for yourself.

∞

MARDUKITE SYSTEMOLOGY SOCIETY ESOTERIC RESEARCH LIBRARY ARCHIVE COLLECTOR'S EDITION HARDCOVERS

Systemology "New Standard" Course Books
Fundamentals of Systemology (Basic Course) [Liber-S1A]
The Pathway to Ascension (2 Volumes) [Liber-5 {5A} + 6 {5B}]
Keys to the Kingdom (2 Volumes) [Liber-7 + 8]

Systemology "Basic Level" Core Research Volumes
The Power of Zu [Liber-S1Z]
Systemology: The Original Thesis [Liber-S1X]
The Way Into The Future [Liber-S1W]

Systemology "Master Level" Core Research Volumes
The Tablets of Destiny Revelation [Liber-One]
Crystal Clear: Handbook for Seekers [Liber-2B]
Metahuman Destinations (2 Volumes) [Liber-2C + 2D]

Systemology "Wizard Level" Core Research Volumes
Imaginomicon [Liber-3D]
The Way of the Wizard [Liber-3E {3}]
Systemology-180: A Fast-Track to Ascension [Liber-180]
Systemology: Backtrack [Liber-4]

NEW STANDARD SYSTEMOLOGY COMPLETE COURSE SCHEDULE

Fundamentals of Systemology (Basic Course)

Lesson #1 – *Being More Than Human*
Lesson #2 – *Realities In Agreement*
Lesson #3 – *Windows to Experience*
Lesson #4 – *Ancient Systemology*
Lesson #5 – *A History of Systemology*
Lesson #6 – *Systemology Processing*

The Pathway to Ascension (Professional Course)

PC#1 – *Increasing Awareness (Level-0)*
PC#2 – *Thought & Emotion (Level-0)*
PC#3 – *Clear Communication (Level-0)*
PC#4 – *Handling Humanity (Level-1)*
PC#5 – *Free Your Spirit (Level-2)*
PC#6 – *Escaping Spirit-Traps (Level-2)*
PC#7 – *Eliminating Barriers (Level-3)*
PC#8 – *Conquest of Illusion (Level-3)*
PC#9 – *Confronting the Past (Level-4)*
PC#10 – *Lifting the Veils (Level-4)*
PC#11 – *Spiritual Implants (Level-5)*
PC#12 – *Games and Universes (Level-5)*
PC#13 – *Spiritual Energy (Level-6)*
PC#14 – *Spiritual Machinery (Level-6)*
PC#15 – *The Arcs of Infinity (Level-6)*
PC#16 – *Alpha Thought (Level-6)*

Keys to the Kingdom (Advanced Training Course)

AT#1 – *The Secret of Universes (Level-7)*
AT#2 – *Games, Goals & Purposes (Level-7)*
AT#3 – *The Jewel of Knowledge (Level-7)*
AT#4 – *Implanted Universes (Level-7)*
AT#5 – *Entities & Fragments (Level-8)*
AT#6 – *Spiritual Perception (Level-8)*
AT#7 – *Mastering Ascension (Level-8)*
AT#8 – *Advancing Systemology (Level-8)*

:: MARDUKITE ACADEMY ::
INTRODUCING NEW STANDARD SYSTEMOLOGY

Mardukite Systemology is a new evolution in Human understanding about the "systems" governing *Life, Reality,* the *Universe* and all *Existences*. It is also a *Spiritual Path* used to transcend the Human experience and reach *"Ascension."*

New Standard Systemology courses are intended to assist *advancing* a *Seeker's* personal progress toward the *upper-most levels* of the *Pathway*.

The systematic methodology that we use to assist an individual to increase their *"Actualized Awareness"* (and reach gradually higher toward their *"Spiritual Ascension"*) is referred to as *"The Pathway"* —and that individual is called a *"Seeker."*

To receive the greatest benefit from this manual: it is expected that a *Seeker* will already be familiar with the fundamental concepts and terminology (previously relayed in the *"Fundamentals of Systemology" Basic Course* and the *"Pathway to Ascension" Professional Course* lessons) of our *applied philosophy*.

As a *Seeker* increases their *Awareness* in this lifetime, their spiritual *"Knowingness"* also increases—which is to say their *certainty* on *Life*, on this and other *Universes*, and on *realizing Self* as an unlimited "spiritual being" *having* an enforced restrictive "human experience." A *Seeker* also *knowingly* increases their command and control of the "human experience." And this is a part of what is meant by *"Actualized Awareness."*

A NEW VIEW OF THE HUMAN SPIRIT

Systemology is not a religion and does not require any type of *faith*. It is, however, built upon a "spiritual" premise—and as such is an "applied spiritual philosophy." It is based on ancient teachings that we are *Spiritual Beings* essentially "wearing" bodies like clothes—or using them as "vehicles." Yet our true native nature is not *physical*, but beyond this existence; and we can certainly operate a "body" from *outside* of it.

We are **all** *Spiritual Beings*—each of us a *unit* of *Spiritual Awareness*—that have experienced a very long *Spiritual Timeline* of existence. Although we might be particularly attached to the familiar "physical shells" associated with *this* lifetime, our true "*Spiritual Lifetime*" is seemingly *eternal*. We have been many things before *Human*, and we go onward as a *Spiritual Being* after our "*genetic vehicle*" of *this* incarnation perishes.

While a "spiritual" view of the *Human Condition* may not seem unique to our philosophy, just how often is the concept treated *systematically*? For that matter: just how many people, supposedly raised to this or that religion, or professing to believe one thing or another, actually live their lives as though they are really *Spirits*?

As *Spiritual Beings* of immortal existence and infinite potential, we are not simply the "*creations*" of an even greater *Beingness*; we are, in fact, an integral part of that "*creative force*" which permeates all existence.

Our basic nature is to be a "*creative being*"—our highest goals are "*to create.*" And as such a being—which we refer to as an *Alpha-Spirit* in *Systemology*—we have run into some difficulties along the course of our *Spiritual Timeline* and found ourselves trapped within material *Universes* of our own collaborative *creation*.

Since we did not start out our existence in a trapped condition, it is correct to say that we have "*fallen*" from our native "*godlike*" states. It did not happen all at one, but progressively and systematically.

We know our "troubles" have resulted from accumulated "barriers" and "blockages"—or *fragmentation*—during our vast experiences as *Spiritual Beings*. They are not because we lack something; but because of what's been added.

In *Systemology*, we systematically examine those routes by which we must have descended to reach our present condition, then reverse the direction of travel and chart a personal "*Pathway to Ascension*." Of course, the exact "details" of the *Spiritual Timeline* will be different for each individual *Seeker*. However, we have been able to systematically chart our *Pathway* based on common patterns of *Human fragmentation*.

In the most basic terms: the *fragmentation* that defines our "downward spiral" consists of decisions or considerations where we deny our true nature. This includes those decisions to "*withdraw*" rather than "*reach*"; where we choose to *not-know* rather than *know*; to *not-communicate* rather than *communicate*; and ultimately, to take *no-responsibility* for being a *creative-cause*, and therefore succumb to being an *effect*.

But there is *hope!* And much more importantly: there is an effectively workable *way out* of the mazes and traps of our existence. If you are reading this now, you have already begun to gather your tools and build up the *"horsepower"* necessary to break the gravity holding your *Spiritual Beingness* to the *Human Condition*.

CHARTING FLIGHTS ON THE PATHWAY

Although there is a systematic structure to *fragmentation*, the personal journey experienced along the *Pathway* will be different for each *Seeker*. For example, certain areas will seem more *"turbulent"* or difficult for one *Seeker* than another. We tend to say that these areas have more *"charge"* on them—or that they are more *"heavily charged."* It is best to handle such areas when you are already feeling "good" and not in a situation (or condition) where that specific area is consistently being *"triggered"* or *"restimulated."*

As an applied philosophy, *Systemology* "theory" can be easily utilized in the "laboratory" of the "world-at-large" in everyday life. This is implied within the basic instruction of each lesson. Unlike other "sciences" that conduct experiments by making a change to some "objective variable" *out there* and waiting to see an effect, our focus is the individual (or *Observer*) themselves, and how *they* affect the *"Reality"* perceived.

Our philosophy is applied by using specific exercises and systematic techniques. These *"processes"* provide the most stable personal gain (and *realizations*) for each area; but only when actually applied with a *Seeker's* full *"presence"* and *Awareness*. Hundreds of such *processes* may be found in the *"Pathway to Ascension"* (*Professional Course*) material.

Applying a technique is called *"running a process."* *Processes* are designed with very simple instructions or *"command-lines."* To *run* a *processing command-line*, a *Seeker* may be assisted by the communication of that *line* from a *"Co-Pilot"* (as in *"Traditional Piloting"*). But even then, a *Seeker* must still personally "input" the *command* as *Self*. For this reason—and quite thankfully—*Solo-Processing* is possible.

TAKING FLIGHT ON THE PATHWAY

Processing Techniques are intended to treat the *Spiritual Being* or *Alpha-Spirit*; the individual themselves. The *"command-lines"* are *directed to* the individual themselves —not some *mental machinery* of theirs, and not even a *Biofeedback* metering device.

Systematic Processing is applied by the *Alpha-Spirit*—who then *Self-directs* command of their "Mind-System" or "body" (*genetic-vehicle*); both of which are "constructs" that the *Alpha-Spirit* (*Self*, or the "I-AM" *Awareness unit*) operates; but neither of which is actually *Self*.

Fragmentation causes *Humans* to falsely identify *Self as* the *"Mind"* or even a *"Body."*

Some *processes* can be treated quite lightly at first; others may require a bit of working at in order to get *"running"* well. It is important to set aside a period of time when you can be dedicated to your studies and *processing*. This period of time is referred to as a *"processing session."*

When a *process* does start *running* well, it is important to be able to complete it to a satisfactory *"end-point."*

Processing allows us to be able to *actually* "look" at *things* and even determine the *considerations* we have made—or attitudes we have decided—about *Reality* as a result of those experiences.

It doesn't do us much good to simply "glance"—or to *restimulate* something uncomfortable and then quickly *withdraw* from it once again, leaving more of our *attention* yet again behind and held fixedly on it.

Generally speaking, a *Seeker* continues to *run* a *process* so long as something is "happening"—which is to say, the *process* is still producing a change. Usually this is evident by the type of "answers" that a *command-line* prompts a *Seeker* to originate from the database of their own *Mind-System*.

The *"Processing Command-Lines"* ("PCL") are not "magic words"; they do not "do" anything on their own. They systematically assist a *Seeker* to selectively direct their own attention toward the increase of *Awareness*.

A *Seeker* may also cease to generate new "data" from a *process* without reaching an *"ultimate" realization* as an *"end-point."* It is possible that additional "layers" (or even other "areas") require handling before anything "deeper" is accessible. If this is the case, end the *process*. But, if a *Seeker* is *withdrawing* from something uncomfortable that was incited or stirred up, then a *process* is *run* until they feel "good" about it.

One of the benefits to *Flying-Solo* on the *Pathway* is that the *processing* is entirely *Self-determined*. This naturally provides a certain built-in "safety" for the practitioner. Anything you *restimulate* by *Self-determinism* is *your thing*. It is not triggered or incited by some external *"other-*

determined" influences (or other "source-points") that make you an *effect*. It can be more easily handled in *processing*—or you can simply let things "cool down" and come back to it again in another *session*.

While it may seem "mysterious" to beginners, a *Seeker* gets a sense for knowing how long to *run* a *process* only with practice.

Once you have spent some time actually applying material from *"The Pathway to Ascension" Professional Course*, there are many aspects of it that become "second nature" because they are, in fact, a part of our true original native nature. All we have done in *Systemology* is *"reverse engineer"* the routes of *creation* and *consideration* that are already *our own*.

YOUR FUTURE & SYSTEMOLOGY

The *New Standard Systemology "Pathway to Ascension Professional Course"* provides training and processing techniques for the entire *Pathway* leading up to the upper-most levels of our *Systemology* work. It consists of *16* progressive lessons—similar in style to the presentation of the *six* lessons of the *"Fundamentals of Systemology" Basic Course*.

Upper-most levels of our *New Standard Systemology* continue after the *"Pathway to Ascension."* Such material is now presented as the *"Keys to the Kingdom" Advanced Training Course*. It consists of *8* progressive manuals that should be studied/used only after a *Seeker*/student has completed the *"Pathway to Ascension"* series.

"Years ago, we realized that '*The Way Out*' would systematically resemble the routes by which we descended. We understood that the '*Gates*' reflected in our most archaic esoteric lore were pointing toward a *realization* that had been lost in translation along the way—and that our only hope of finding a *Map* to this *Pathway* was in recovering that lost understanding. I believe that our Systemology is successfully delivering a communication that is unparalleled in today's society—and most of you here can attest that: above and beyond the former gradients of knowledge available to us in our world, this work we are doing now is our best chance at 'making the grade' to reach our *Metahuman Ascension* in *this* lifetime; and for the first time in a very long time, reclaim the true power of the *Alpha-Spirit* and the freedom to experience an existence of our own true *Self-determined* creation."

—*Joshua Free, <u>Backtrack Lectures</u>*

INTRODUCTION TO SYSTEMOLOGY PROCESSING

FUNDAMENTALS BASIC COURSE LESSON-6
PRACTICES OF SPIRITUAL AWAKENING

The philosophy of *Systemology* may be applied to many fields and areas of everyday life. When *applied* within our tradition, practices and exercises toward "spiritual awakening"—or the *"Pathway to Ascension"*—are referred to as *"systematic processing."* [Some of the inspiration behind this is derived from sources highlighted in *Basic Course "Lesson 5."* But really this new standard is the product of many years and innumerable sources.]

"Systematic Processing" is only *one* part of our philosophy. It is itself an entire "methodology" for applying *Systemology* as a personal practice of techniques and exercises. We call it *"systematic processing"* because it is a precise practice (or "ritual") that *knowingly* mirrors or duplicates the "systematic processes" of the *Mind*. It is too broad a topic to cover fully in a *Basic Course* lesson (booklet), but we can introduce its practice.

One of the basic goals of *"processing"* is to treat *knowingly* (at an analytical level of *awareness*) what is happening "automatically" or "compulsively"—or otherwise *unknowingly*. However, *processing* may be better understood as "techniques" or "technology" aimed toward "spiritual development" and "ability enhancement." Of course, these *processes* or techniques are *applications* based on our *philosophy*. Hence our work is an "applied philosophy."

Effectiveness of *systematic processing* is entirely based on our principle axiom that: The "I" or *Self* is an *Alpha-Spirit* operating from a *Spiritual ("Alpha") Existence* and employing a *Mind-System* to perceive the sensory experience of a *genetic-vehicle* (or '*body*') that interacts in a *Physical ("Beta") Existence*. This axiom *is* "The" primary *Fundamental of Systemology*—as already introduced throughout the previous *Basic Course* lessons (booklets).

Systematic Processing does resemble some practices from our predecessors in history; perhaps because it reaches for some of the same goals and ideals. It is, however, *not* synonymous with (or equivalent to) these other methods —meditation, prayer, mental healing, therapy, psychoanalysis, *&tc.*—at least not as they are commonly understood by the general (*exoteric*) public. Therefore, we tend to avoid using such terminology.

The most common application of *Systemology* is "*defragmentation*"—but this is only *one* use of "*processing.*" *Defragmentation* is best understood with the model of "*knowns* versus *not-knowns*" given in the introduction. While many assume this means only a *knowledge* of "facts," the same example could illustrate other uses of *processing*, such as a gradual increase of "dormant" (or forgotten) "*spiritual ability*" into "*actual ability*" *&tc.*

BASIC METHODS OF PROCESSING

An "applied philosophy" is really only as effective as an individual *understands* that philosophy and is able to *apply* it in practice. If a *Seeker* is unable to *understand* the philosophy enough to *apply* it, the logical solution is to find an individual that is professionally trained to *understand* it, until the *Seeker* has a *reality* on it themselves. For this, we developed the idea of a *"Pilot"* that could assist in guiding a *Seeker* on the *Pathway*.

This *"Pilot"* concept led to three basic "methods" of *systematic processing*, originally distinguished as *Piloted*, *Co-Piloted* and *Flying-Solo*. Over the course of many years of additional work, the meaning implied by these terms has evolved slightly during development. But, to briefly describe, they are:

Piloted Processing—an untrained *Seeker* is processed by a professionally trained *"Pilot."*

Co-Piloted Processing—two *Seekers* in training take turns processing one another; or a *Seeker* is processed by a trusted friend, reading from a book.

Flying-Solo—a *Seeker* in training processes themselves.

When first established in the 2010's, all *systematic processing* was intended to be *"Piloted"*—administered by a book-trained or Academy-trained *"Pilot"*—or *"Co-Piloted"* with a friend, or fellow *Seeker*, as *"Pilots-in-Training."* And this is exactly how *"Route-1"* (the first experimental method of *processing*) is presented in *"Tablets of Destiny Revelation"* (2019). More recently, *"Co-Piloted"* seems to apply to anything not done *"Solo."*

Soon after our debut publication, we realized the obvious limitations of a strictly *(Co-)Piloted* approach. We decided that when we developed additional routes, they would need to apply to both traditional *"Piloting"* and solitary practitioners (who were *"Flying Solo"*). That being said, there *are* some *processes* (such as *"Route-1"*) that greatly benefit from having another individual present; yet others are just as productive when "run" *Solo*.

A *Seeker* working alone has only the option of being their own *Solo Pilot*. As such, they are responsible for all the "training" as a *Pilot*, and also managing the "*processing session*" for themselves as a *Seeker*. A certain level of *Self-Determinism* and *Actualized Awareness* must already be in place in order to successfully "*Fly Solo*," since no one else is *present* to help maintain a *Seeker's* "*presence*" (*attention* and *Awareness*) *in session*.

The phrase "*Self-Processing*" is sometimes used in place of "*Solo*"—but this is not necessarily the most accurate term. Whether a *Seeker* is practicing alone or not, all *systematic processing* techniques in *Systemology* are "*Self-processed*"—which is to say, they must be *processed* by *Self*. And if it seems to you that *Systemology is* sometimes talking about software programming, or operating a computer, you're not alone; but it works.

A *Pilot* may assist in directing attention—or "redirecting" attention, if it strays—but the "command line" (verbal instruction) of a *process* is not a "magic spell" that "does something" by itself. To be effective, the *Seeker* must actually *apply* the "command line" of the technique as *Self* to *Self*. This is what we mean by "running a process"—because essentially, a *Seeker* is *processing* the "command" and resulting *data* as *Self*.

SYSTEMATIC PROCESSING SESSIONS

New "*realizations*" and increased *Actualized Awareness* improve a *Seeker's* handling of everyday life. This may be enhanced through educational training, but a more effective means of reaching these higher ideal states is by combining book-learning with actual practice of the *Systemology* techniques and experiencing the exercises we refer to as *"systematic processing."* A few of these have already appeared in previous *Basic Course* lessons.

To be strictly technical, the practice of *systematic processing* is conducted in a formal *"session."* We prefer the term "session" because of the common mystical and/or religious connotations associated with the word *"ritual"*—or even *"meditation."* Our use of the phrase *"processing session"* is most accurate since it implies a specific duration of uninterrupted time set aside to focus on a particular procedure—or *process*.

Rather than conceiving the idea of a "session" as being similar to some "hourly counseling" in some other tradition, a "session" is a period of time for "running a process" toward an intended result or "end-point." A single "session" could last twenty minutes or two hours or more (taking breaks as needed, of course).

Proper procedures for conducting a "session" are followed whether a *Seeker* is *Solo* or *Co-Piloted*. This allows a *Seeker* to treat *systematic processing* as its own unique activity. For example: *"bathing"* is its own unique activity; but it also carries with it a whole regimen of "steps" that are followed in sequence—and which eventually become *"routine"* to the *process*. A *Seeker* practices to achieve that same level of familiarity.

That being said: even the fundamental practice of "starting a session," providing *"presence"* (*attention* and *Awareness*) to be "in session," then formally "ending the session," is a *systematic procedure* or *routine* in itself. To ensure effective processing, we add a step to getting *"in session."* A *Seeker* "scans through daily life" for upsets or problems that are "holding" parts of their *attention* or *Awareness*, even if only on the periphery.

When *things* are not handled analytically—or "above the surface"—they remain in suspension. A *thing* does not *disappear* by our withdrawing from it; it waits around, albeit out of view, to be seen *"As-It-Is."* Many aspects of living out the *Human Condition* have a tendency to keep our *attention* suspended. Even when we go about performing other actions, the totality of our available *Awareness* is not generally present.

For example: we might be preparing a meal for our family, but at the same time we are thinking about problems at work, difficulties in managing the bills, and the driver that almost collided with us on the way home. It is also at these moments, when not living deliberately, that accidents can occur—because, the individual "isn't there" or their "mind isn't on it." Either way, they have withdrawn part of their *"presence."*

Applying *"presence"* to a session is one of the most critical fundamentals of *processing*. Without it, a *Seeker* is not actually *"present"* to be *processed.* We aren't interested in *processing* a "body" or "computer-mind"; we are communicating directly with *Self*, the *Alpha-Spirit* that *utilizes* a *"Mind"* and *"Body"*—and *Self* maintains a "spiritual identity" that is independent of a *"Mind"* and *"Body."* It is *Self* that we want *present* in session.

Systematic Processing operates by taking *knowing control* of an individual's available *Actualized Awareness* and then increasing it—both the level of *control* and the available *Awareness*. This is similar to taking a small amount of *cer-*

tainty or *ability* and "building up" from there. For a *processing session* to be effective, a *Seeker* cannot be withdrawing their *"presence"*—distracted by the upsets of daily life. This must be handled first.

It is no great mystery that having part of our *attention* on all of the aspects of living (that we hold at length on the peripheral boundary of our conscious *Awareness*) might inhibit our focused concentration or the achievement (or experience) of other "states." But, we can't simply ignore this fact, telling our *Seekers* and readers that we hope they feel better one day and come back to us when they do. We handle it *in-session*.

HANDLING IN-SESSION PRESENCE

Establishing *"in-session presence"* is not simply a preliminary step; it is a *systematic procedure* in itself. In fact, it is actually the *single* element underlying all other practices —of meditation, prayer, ritualism, *&tc.*—that produces any real *effects*. Of course, in other practices, these *effects* are misappropriated to some other *cause*.

The "location"—the environment or "setting"—is one of the first things to consider for establishing a session. This may be in an uninterrupted space outdoors, or in a quiet room. On occasion, the instruction or "command line" of a *process* may be directed toward a particular environmental focus—such as an "item" *in the room*, or a "person" engaged with others in a *public place.* These are indicators of the intended *setting*.

With the *setting* identified, the next step is making certain a *Seeker* is comfortable and relaxed within that environment. It is unproductive to attempt *processing* in an environment that is actively a source of "turbulence"—or worse, the very type of turbulence that is going to be *processed*. There is no reason for some cult-like disconnection; but a *Seeker* should have a *"retreat"* available to them while regaining balance.

Once a "safe location" is available, our next concern is the *Seeker's* comfort and familiarity with the material and intended practice. In traditional *Piloting*, this would include not only a confidence in the philosophy, but also the individual (*"Pilot"*) administering it. When applied to a *Seeker* that is not also in-training, the total control of *processing* must be handled by a *Pilot* until the *Seeker* assumes responsibility for that control.

All of these factors boil down to what we consider the first elements of *"in-session presence"* that a *Seeker* provides to their exercises (*processing*)—the *attention* that they have available and are willing to provide to the session *in* present-time. And when we say *"presence,"* we mean, quite literally, the *Awareness* of actually *"being present"* in the session. This *"presence" is* the unifying factor of all effective spiritual practices.

Other factors being considered, the actual "orientation" of a *Seeker's presence*—present-time *Awareness*—*with* the present space-time *setting* or environment, is the primary "opening procedure" for a *processing session.* An integral part of this procedure is determining if there are any aspects from daily life that are *inhibiting presence*. Sometimes the handling of these aspects alone is enough to qualify a complete session.

A *Seeker* handles the upsets or energetic-turbulence that is already present—or in stimulation—on the *ZU-Line* before attempting to *resurface* or reveal additional layers of *fragmentation*. Energy is always relayed as a "communication" (even internally for our *"perceptions"*); therefore, most upsets can be categorized as a type of "communication-breakdown" or "break in reality"—an unexpected interruption in the energy *flow*.

Different *processing* techniques target specific aspects of life. But, as a general rule—and in regards to *presence*—the basic idea is to *confront* ("come around to face") or *reach* rather than *avoid* or *withdraw*. Those *things* that we have 'blanked out'—or choose not to look at—are still "energetic masses" surrounding our "field" of *Awareness*. All a *Seeker* really needs to do is *"acknowledge"* they exist so *attention* can shift off them.

To approach this *systematically*, a *Seeker* "spots" whatever incident or aspect is bothering them, then *looks* it over carefully and *analytically*. This may be done as thoroughly as is needed—noticing various things about it, but essentially *acknowledging* or *confronting* a thing *"As-It-Is."* This allows a *Seeker* to put some distance between themselves and the energetic-mass (*"problem"*) rather than treating it as though it were "present."

We return to our previous example of worrying about things while preparing a meal, even if *unknowingly*, which leads to an accident. What is taking place is that the individual is treating those other things as though they are *present* in the environment—giving them "attention- units" as though they are an imminent threat. Of course, by agreement, they are *real things, real incidents*, but *are* they actually *"present" in session?*

Once a troublesome aspect or incident is analyzed (as above), there should be some feeling of relief and an ability to refocus *attention* and *presence in-session*. A "problem" should *seem* "further" away (rather than overwhelmingly close). If this is not the case, there may be another upset or distraction. If the troublesome aspect *seems* closer, then alternate *looking* at something in the incident and something in your environment.

This brings us to the other part of establishing *presence in-session*, which is "orientation with the present space-time" (or environment). Essentially, this is a part of what a *Seeker* is employing when *attention* is alternated by *looking* at something in the incident or situation and then something in the physical surroundings. We employ a similar technique as an "opening procedure" for all formal sessions as well.

In the case of handling "problems" or upsets, the alternation allows a *Seeker* to "unfix" *unknowing attention* on something that is being "fixedly" treated as "present" (*in-the-now*) when it is really *somewhere* else or a *past* situation no longer happening presently. These aspects that *attention* is *unknowingly* "fixed" to are what reduces available *Actualized Awareness* that is applied to any "present-time" activity—including *processing*.

Once *Awareness* is able to be focused or concentrated, this additional step—"orientation with present space-time" is essentially exactly what it sounds like: "orienting" *Self* in the present time and space of the session. This means bringing total available *Awareness* to the present-time location (space) of the session and the control of the "body" *in-session*. With regular practice these steps take less time further along the *Pathway*.

The experience of *"Presence In-Session"* will be familiar to continuing students and readers. Versions of sample techniques used in "opening procedures" of a *"Formal Session"* are given in previous *Fundamentals of Systemology Basic Course* lessons (booklets) as follows:

Lesson 1, Exercise *1* and *2*;

Lesson 2, Exercise *1* and *7*;

Lesson 3, Exercise *1, 2* and *7*.

THE FORMAL SESSION

All *systematic processing* is practiced as part of a *"formal" systematic processing session*. Of course, there are some exercises—such as those included at the end of each lesson (booklet)—that are effective even when practiced on their own. However, whether *Solo* or *Co-Piloted*, a *Seeker* applying our methods as a total *Pathway* toward *Spiritual Awakening* (or *"Ascension"*), benefits most by practicing techniques *systematically*.

A session is considered *"formal"* because it follows a specific pattern or ceremonial formula of *formal* action and communication. There is a *formal* "beginning" and "ending" of a *systematic session*. Several *processes* may occur within a single session; each one "started" and "stopped" (in turn) as a *formal* act.

Traditional *Piloted Processing* differs from *Flying-Solo*, but the basic formula for a *"Formal Session"* is the same. In *Piloted* (or *Co-Piloted*) *processing*, the factor of *communication* between a *Pilot* and *Seeker* must be handled in addition to the *session* and *processes*. In *Solo-Processing*, the *communication* of a *process in-session* is all handled "internally"—between *Self* and the *"Mind"* (and *"Body"*) without being directed by a *"Co-Pilot."*

A precise instruction for a *process* is referred to as a *"processing command line"* (or "PCL"). This is named for the act of "inputting" a "command line" into a "computing device." In traditional *Piloted* sessions, a *Seeker* receives a communicated "command line" from the *Pilot*, then communicates the "command" to the *Mind* as *Self*. *Solo* or not, a *Seeker* directs their own *Mind* to *process* the "command"; another *Pilot* only assists this.

A *"processing command line"* (PCL), by itself, is *not* a "magical incantation" that spontaneously produces *actualization*. A misunderstood one, however, *does* have the "power" to slow or stop forward progress. A *Seeker* that is studying/training on their own usually does not have an issue *in-session*, because they can get a clear understanding beforehand. A *Pilot* is responsible for making sure of this for a *Seeker* not in-training.

For example: if you take someone randomly off the street and ask, *"would it be okay if we start this session?"* Well, there is obviously little context there. Even an individual that is interested in getting *processed* might not understand the use of the word "session" at first unless some of the basic *Systemology* philosophy is explained. A *Solo-Pilot* simply accepts total responsibility for attaining this understanding for themselves.

Solo-Sessions may be run *"silently"* as direct "mental commands"—but this is not an absolute rule. In either case, a *Seeker* should be focused on handling the commands directly and not *imagine* also *being* "another person" that is giving themselves the commands. Such "add-ons" are unnecessary and counter-productive. However, the same formal session "script" that a *Co-Pilot* communicates, a *Solo-Pilot* reads and *Self-Directs*.

The whole purpose of a *processing session* surrounds the idea of an individual focusing and increasing their *Self-directed* control—or *Self-determinism*. In order to retain this focus, every *one* PCL of a formal session or *process* must have a *Seeker's* total *presence*. This level of focused direction is one benefit of traditional *Piloting*—but in *Solo*, a *Seeker* is instructed to keep a piece of paper over portions of a script/process not yet used.

What follows is a basic script from a *Formal Session* used for training purposes at the Academy. It is a guideline only—based on a transcript of a traditional *Piloted Processing Session*. It is, however, easily adapted to use for *Flying-Solo* once a *Seeker* has practiced the exercises used for achieving *presence in-session*.

1. BEGINNING THE SESSION

"Would it be okay with you if we begin this session now?"

"Okay."

"Start of session."

2. OPENING PROCEDURES

  A. Presence In-Session

"Is there anything going on that might keep your attention from being present in-session?"

  (if *"no,"* acknowledge and go to *B.*; if *"yes,"* continue below)

"Okay. Tell me about it."

"Alright. How does that problem seem to you now?"

(if *"further away"* or handled, acknowledge and go to B.; if *"closer"* or more turbulent, continue below)

"Spot something in the incident; Spot something in the room."

(this alternating command line is repeated as needed)

B. Orientation in Present Space-Time

"Get the sense of you making that body sit in that chair."

"Okay. Get a sense of the floor beneath your feet."

"Do you have that real good?"

(if *"no,"* acknowledge and repeat A.; if *"yes,"* continue below)

"Recall a time something seemed real to you."

"Tell me something you notice about it."

"Look around and spot something in the room."

"What do you notice about that?"

(these last four command lines are repeated in series as needed; acknowledge and continue below)

C. Control of Body and Mind In-Session

(two dissimilar objects—here given as *"Item-1"* and *"Item-2"*—are presented and placed within reach; or alternatively, at two distant points in the room, in which a command line for "walking" between them would be inserted)

"Pick up Item-1."

"Tell me about its weight."

"Tell me about its color."

"Tell me about its texture."

"Put it down."

"Pick up Item-2."

"Tell me about its weight."

"Tell me about its color."

"Tell me about its texture."

"Put it down."

(this series of command-lines may be repeated several times; when there is no communication-lag for several full series, and duplicate answers are reoccurring, acknowledge and continue below)

"Choose an object. Decide when you are going to reach for it. Then make that body pick it up."

"Now decide when you are going to put it down. Then make that body put it back where it was."

(repeat as needed; when there is no communication-lag for a full series of command lines, acknowledge and continue below)

"Close your eyes. Put all of your attention on the upper two back corners of the room and just get real interested in them for a while."

(if there are no visible signs of "strain" after two minutes, acknowledge and continue below)

D. Establishing the Session

"Do you have any goals for this session, or anything in particular you want to address?"

(acknowledge, then start a process)

3. STARTING A PROCESS

"I would like to start a process; would that be okay?"

"Alright. The command lines are ---. Does this make sense?"

(if *"no,"* clear up any misunderstood words; if *"yes,"* start the process)

4. CHANGING A PROCESS

(only the wording in a command line may be changed to make it more workable for a *Seeker*; to change processes altogether, the present process must reach an end-point)

Example: a Seeker expresses inability to "imagine" or visualize imagery.

"Okay. Well, just 'get a sense' of..." or *"Just 'get the idea' of..."*

Example: a Seeker expresses discomfort (or withdrawal from) recalling a particular incident.

"That's fine. What part of that incident 'could' you confront?"

5. STOPPING A PROCESS

(when an end-point has been reached on a repetitive-style process)

"We'll just run this process a couple more times if that's okay with you?"

(general process is run two more times)

"Okay. Is there anything you would like to tell me before we end this process?"

(**or**, if an end-point "realization" is communicated from a process)

"Alright. Very good."

(the formal end of a particular process requires a command-line)

"End of process."

6. ENDING THE SESSION

(once a process, or series of processes, is completed)

"Is there anything you would like to tell me before we end this session?"

(if *"yes,"* acknowledge and handle it with communication before ending the session; if *"no,"* continue below)

"Would it be okay if we ended this session now?"

"Okay. End of session."

SYSTEMOLOGY PILOTING MANUAL

SYSTEMATIC PROCESSING

Systematic Processing is primarily about *looking* and *seeing* "*What Is*"—*As-It-Is*. "*Processing Command Lines*" (or "PCL") are really a query-line (or question) of "*what is*"? The response is based on whatever our *attention* (*Awareness*) is on, or directed to. Even when not worded as a literal question, a PCL is still a prompt for such a response. For example:

Q: *Recall a time when... (What is it?)*
A: *(It is) when such-and-such...*

Q: *Spot something in the... (What is it?)*
A: *(It is) that thing...*

Q: *Notice something about... (What is it?)*
A: *(It is) this...*

A *Seeker* is still permitted to *consider* or *wonder about* things. But to avoid having progress slow down to a halt during a *processing session*: the focus should be on what they *can identify*, *see*, or *know about*, rather than concentrating on "*unknowns*."

To be effective, *systematic processing* is applied to only one thing/area at a time. It is for this reason that a *Pilot* must be aware of where a *Seeker's attention* is *fixed*—or a *Solo-Pilot* must be aware of it.

If *attention is* "stuck" on a point that can't be put aside, then it must be addressed first in *processing*, because that is the *fixed* point of *attention* that all other *processing* will take place from anyways. The "*presence*" that is elsewhere must be brought under *control* before other gains will be made "*in-session*."

Defragmentation is a gradual process of relieving the "weight" off of the *Spirit*. This "weight" is mostly *persistently created entangled energy-masses*. A proper "session" should provide *some sense of release* to a *Seeker* for it to be effective.

If a *process* is not *run long enough*, there is a general feeling of "incompleteness." A *Seeker* may feel irritable as a result. Irritability and hopeless feelings are good indicators for a *process* being *"under-run."* The solution is to *run* the *process* longer.

The other side of this—*"over-run"*—tends to make things more *"solid"* or feel *"heavier."* Usually an area or target item was *defragmented* (a *release-point* was achieved) but since the *process* continues to target it as *being there*, it gets "pulled in" again, or else is *recreated*. This often happens when a beginner expects a single *process* to handle everything, or do it all, when it really requires applying many different *processes*, each providing another step forward as a fairly quick progression.

The *systematic* solution to an *"over-run" process* is to simply *"spot"* and *acknowledge* the point when the *"win"* or *"new realization"* had occurred (but was overlooked, not *acknowledged*, and *invalidated*).

PREVENTATIVE FUNDAMENTALS

If a *Seeker* has an *upset*, a *problem*, or any *attention* "stuck" on things they are worried about, it is not possible to progress in other areas until this handled. In the *Professional Course*, this handling is called "preventative fundamentals" because a *Pilot* must take care of these things first before attempting to spend *session* time in other areas. What we are *preventing* is an *invalidation* of our methods by a *Seeker* that is unable to apply *presence* of *attention in-session*. These fundamentals are treated in *Professional Course* materials:

1. A *break* or *upset* in the "*Flow-Factors*" —enforced or inhibited *communication, likingness* and/or *agreement*. [*PC Lesson-7, "Eliminating Barriers"*]

2. A "*Human Problem*" —present-time *attention* (*presence*) is occupied fixedly elsewhere (and outside one's own control). [*PC Lesson-4, "Handling Humanity"*]

3. A "*Hold-Out*" —*attention* restimulated an area, usually because someone else *almost found out* about it. [*PC Lesson-6, "Escaping Spirit-Traps"*]

A *Solo-Pilot* looks over this list and determines if any of these factors are in play at the start of a *session*. In *Traditional Piloting*, a *GSR-Meter* may be used to *assess* if anything on the list *reads*. For example:

1. "Is there a *break* or *upset* of a *Flow-Factor?*"

[if it "*reads*," check]

   a. "Is there a break in *Communication?*"

   b. "On *Likingness?*"

   c. "On *Agreement?*"

[then, *run* on which of *a, b,* or *c,* "*reads*"]

   a. "Was this ___ *Enforced?*"

   b. "*Inhibited?*"

In this first case: when you can *spot* the primary underlying source of the *upset*—such as "*inhibited communication*" or "*enforced agreement*"—there should be *some* feeling of "*relief*." If not: you may need to *reassess* the list.

The *"relief on spotting"* is either partial or total. If total: *acknowledge* it and continue on with the *session*. If partial: handle the *upset* (or *flow-break*) before continuing. It is handled by *spotting* the *flow* and *circuit*.

For example: did *you inhibit (or enforce) someone else's communication (&tc.)* or did *someone else inhibit yours?* Perhaps it was observing *someone else inhibiting another.* Whatever the case: *identify it,* then *spot* exactly what *communication* was *inhibited.* Then *spot* yourself in the situation; what you *did* and *decided* as a result of it, *&tc*. If the *turbulence* doesn't resolve or worsens: look for an earlier incident that was similar. If it gets more *solid,* it has been *over-run*: *spot* the *release-point* that was missed.

TRADITIONAL PILOTING

This manual is a continuation of material presented in *"Systemology Procedures"* and *"Systemology Biofeedback."* Its emphasis is *how to "Pilot"* (or *"Co-Pilot") Systemology* for traditional/professional applications. This is not a guide for *"what to process"* or *"what processing is"*—as such subjects are taken up in other manuals and lessons.

The purpose of this manual is to "pull together" all the data into an applied practice of *helping others—processing others.* There are *no* "special cases" in *Systemology.* We apply *New Standard Systemology*—given in *"Pathway to Ascension" Level-0 to 6;* and *"Keys to the Kingdom" Level-7 and 8*—from *bottom to the top,* to *all Seekers.* To deliver *processing-levels 0-to-6,* a *Pilot* must be *Level-7* or *8,* themselves. Only a *Pilot* that has completed *Level-8* is qualified to supervise paperwork for a *Solo Level-7.*

We originally developed *systematic processing* to train *Mardukite Ministers (of Zuism)* with skills to provide *spiritual advisement* or *counseling*. Initially, there was no prescribed *Pathway*. A *minister* studied our entire philosophy so they could apply the most relevant elements to handle the immediate concerns of an individual coming to them for assistance.

The very first *"Professional Piloting Course"*—from *2020*—is contained in the *"Metahuman Destinations"* volumes. It was there that the "seeds" of a *standardized Pathway* first began to grow; and the basic outline for a *"Formal Session"* began to emerge. It remains our basic *Pilot Training* material.

It is important to handle the immediate concerns of an individual before attempting to guide them along the *Pathway*. If the difficulties and upsets are not treated, then a *"hidden standard"* develops where *Systemology* is only considered to "work" *if* such-and-such a *"condition"* improves.

To effectively *process* another individual, a *Pilot* must apply *Systemology* with *certainty*—of the materials; of their own skill to communicate *processing command lines* (PCL); and their own ability to maintain control of the *systematic processing session*.

A *Pilot* develops their skill similar to how a *Seeker* ascends the *Pathway*; except in this case, the emphasis becomes applying the material to *someone else*, not just *Self*. For example: *Level-0* for the *Pathway* is *"communication."* *Level-0* for *Pilot Training* is also *"communication."* *Clear communication* is necessary for *all processing* to occur.

Piloting requires the *ability-to-confront* the *Seeker* existing across from you in *session*; just as the *Seeker* must be able to *recognize/confront* you as a *Pilot* for the *session*.

It requires an *ability-to-communicate* (project) PCL to a *Seeker* (clearly and directly with *intention*); and see that it has been received, or perceive the response; and then end the *communication-cycle* with an appropriate *acknowledgment*. [These are the same steps a *Seeker* practices on "objects" during *Level-8* (see *AT#7*).]

Traditional Piloting requires the same level of *presence-in-session* described in the *Professional Course* (PC) material of *"Pathway to Ascension."* A *Seeker* has to have *reality* on the *session* for it to be effective. When you say *"recall a time you communicated...,"* does the *Seeker* properly receive, understand, and *process* the *command-line*? Does the *Seeker* even have any *reality* on *Life*; any *reality* on *communicating* at all? You will know by the *communication-lag*; the delay in getting a response or answer—and I mean an actual answer to the PCL; not just the production of a sound.

A *Pilot* must study *Systemology* to have any *reality* on it—otherwise, what are they delivering? If a *Pilot* hasn't gone through *processing* themselves, how are they to understand a *Seeker's* responses?

Traditional Piloting is not a "cultish" tactic; it cannot be enforced. It requires *two-way communication* with a willing *Seeker* that is interested in *Systemology* and their own case—or resolving the *Human Condition*. *Pilot Training* is as much about *communication* and *control* as it is about *processes* and techniques.

A *Pilot* must be able to skillfully deliver *systematic processing*:

—without *Evaluating* out loud to the *Seeker* about things that they should arrive at as their own *end-realizations*;

—without *Invalidating* with disbelief or suppression in any way, or trying to "correct" the data that a *Seeker* is giving; and

—without *Reacting* (or displaying any *emotion*) to anything a *Seeker* says or does during a *session*.

You don't say to a *Seeker*, "*Oh, this is what is going on with you.*" We want the *Seeker* to realize the "*This is..*" part on their own.

ELEMENTS OF PILOTING

There are only four components to *Traditional Piloting*: the *Pilot*; a *Seeker* to *process*; the *session*, or *space* to have a *session*; and the *processing* or *processes*. That's all.

There is a big difference between *talking* and *being in-session* or *processing*. A *Seeker* needs to accept the *Pilot* as their "guide" (or as a *Co-Pilot*) if their presence is to be of any actual assistance to them. We start off, asking: "*Is it alright if I process you?*" And an initial line of communication is established. That's *Level-0*, or *square-one*.

We move on to the next requirement: and that is *presence-in-session*. Is the *Seeker's attention* somewhere other than the *session*? If it is, you aren't going to make any real progress. Whatever a *Seeker's attention* is *fixed* on is considered a "*problem*" to them—that's why they're *fixated* on it.

When a *Seeker* isn't able to apply *presence-in-session*, it is because they are treating something else as happening "now" in the *session*-space *and* time; even when it is not. You can even address this: *"Is this problem happening here in this room?"* or *"Is this person here in this room?"* You could even repeatedly alternate: *"Where is the problem?"* and *"Where are you now?"*

"Human Problems" is treated as *Level-1* on the *Pathway*; and it is *Level-1* for a *Pilot*. In this case, it is the matter of *presence-of- Awareness in-session* for *processing*. There is no progress—no *processing* taking place—if the *Seeker* isn't *present*. You aren't there to *communicate* with their *mental machinery*; you want to *process* a *Seeker*.

At the start of the *session*, you want to determine if a *Seeker's attention* is elsewhere; so you just ask: *"Is there anything that you are currently worried about?"* or *"Is there anything your attention is currently on?"*

New Standard Systemology is already designed for use by *Solo-Pilots*. Therefore, a *Professional Pilot* needs to demonstrate that they are of genuine benefit as an assistant to the *Seeker* on the *Pathway*. You aren't there just to read a book to them.

A *Pilot* ensures there is *presence-in-session* and a *communication-line* before *running* any other *processing*. Obviously, there are *techniques* and *processes* used to accomplish these basic points. But, for example, a *Pilot* isn't going to apply more *"subjective-styled processes"* regarding something that they can't visibly observe, unless they know the *Seeker* can receive PCL and follow commands regarding things that *can* be observed.

If a *Pilot* is having issues with getting a *Seeker* to focus *in-session*, or understand and follow-through with "picking up an object," don't start introverting the *Seeker* to *ima-*

gine/create or *recall* things with any *reality*; because they don't have it (*reality*).

A *"condition"* is a set of circumstances encountered by *Life*—by the *Alpha-Spirit*—and in our work, we are predominantly concerned with the *"Human Condition"*; the *mental-circuitry* and *reality-agreements* associated with the *"Human Condition."*

When handling the *conditions* of *Life*, an individual has two choices: to *increase* or *decrease* their level of *Actualized Awareness*. An individually is either *knowingly direct* in *confronting reality "As-It-Is"* or they are operating *unknowingly, compulsively* and on *automatic*. As a route of *Self-improvement*—or when applied vocationally by a *minister* —*systematic processing* is only *piloted* (or *Co-Piloted*) to assist the *Seeker* in rehabilitating their own abilities.

The *Pathway* is marked by an increased *ability-to-confront* —leading to upper-level abilities of *"defragmentation-by-realization"* alone. It is also critical for a *Pilot* to be able to *confront/handle* the *processing-session*—and the *Seeker* within that *session*.

This means maintaining sufficient control over the *session* and *communication-line* until the *Seeker* can exercise true *Self-Honest* control of focused *attention* and their own *Self-Directed Actualized Awareness*.

Whether or not a *Seeker* is *Co-Piloted* up the *Pathway* through *processing level-6*, the upper-most levels are always handled *"Solo."* This means at some point, a *Seeker* must take total responsibility for their own case. Records of this work can be reviewed by an experienced *Seeker*, but they act solely as an adviser to the *Seeker* in between *Solo-sessions*.

It is difficult for a *Seeker* to apply *presence-in-session*, or work their way along the *Pathway* (*processing-levels 0-to-6*), if they are currently concerned with "pain management" (especially chronic conditions).

Ideally, a *Seeker* becomes more able to *confront* past-incidents and is less likely to *compulsively* (*unknowingly*) create reactive *mental-images* and other *stored impressions* (possibly even at a cellular-level). [More details on this are given in the companion supplement, "*Systemology Procedures.*"]

PILOTING SEEKERS

To apply the *Pathway* material for *Self-improvement*, a *Seeker* needs to feel safe in their environment; and free to *communicate* and *process* without inhibition. They can't be worried that the "*Pilot might find out something.*" It is likely a *Seeker* is carrying around some bad experiences (which is to say *imprints*) concerning *communication* and *contact* with their *environment*.

It is up to a *Pilot* to provide reassurance. You might direct a *Seeker* to: "*Look around the room and spot things that are not being a threat*" or "*...not threatening you.*" Ideally, the *Seeker* will also include "*The Pilot*" in their list of such observations.

Any technique that puts the *Seeker* in contact (*communication*) with their present environment is useful for achieving and maintaining *presence-in-session*, while at the same time, increasing *clear perception* and *Actualized Awareness*.

When a *Seeker* enters upon the *Pathway* from the *Human Condition*, they are *seeking* the *answer* to an ultimate "WHY?"—an ultimate "*Cause Of*"—and they are not going to be able to accept or understand the *answer*—the *Truth*—until it is fully and personally *recognized* and *realized* for what it is. And there certainly *are answers* when a *Seeker* is ready to receive them.

Even the degree to which a *Seeker*, themselves, is actually at *Cause*, is not likely to be accepted early on. Most elements that a *Seeker* believes to be their issue are misassigned or misidentified until they are able to realize their own true *Beingness*—being at *Cause*—and their participation in the *duplication* and *cross-copying* of *reality*.

This *realization* of *total responsibility* is a steep gradient to achieve—and it is not expected all-at-once. In fact, most of the background story of *this Universe* and the *Spiritual Timeline* (or *Backtrack*) of the *Alpha-Spirit* is not totally understood until the *upper-level A.T.* work. But it is *there now*, as the "*Keys to the Kingdom*" series of *advanced training manuals*. It is something we have not kept locked away from you.

Prior to *New Standard Systemology*, the common starting-point was *incident-running*—what we now treat as "*Confronting the Past*" in *PC Lesson-9* (*Level-4*). The first presentation of this appears in "*The Tablets of Destiny Revelation*" (*Liber-One*) as "*Route-1*" or "*Route-1R*." This had mixed results in the very beginning; since it required expert *Piloting* to apply, and there was no existing *Pilot Training* available.

We saw better results after publication of "*Crystal Clear: Handbook for Seekers*"—and it is still just as relevant today even with the *New Standard* that is now available.

If handled earlier on the *Pathway* then *Level-4*, *"confronting-the-past"* or *"incident-running"* (as a *counseling-action*) still requires expert *Piloting*. Even in this case, one can only expect to *destimulate* the area enough to treat with proper *processing* as a part of the greater *Pathway*. Sometimes too much is expected from the techniques early on; as if they are like a *"magic spell."*

Full or *Total Defragmentation* only occurs when the *Alpha Thought*—the *"postulates"* and *"considerations"*—associated with the *incident* (or *imprint*) is *realized* and *confronted "As-It-Is."* This ultimate level of *defragmentation* may not occur early on the *Pathway*—or if techniques are sporadically applied only as *"counseling-actions."*

ENTRY-POINTS TO A SESSION

The *entry-points* of any *case* are the same whether a *Pilot* is going to be able to take a *Seeker* all the way up the *Pathway* or not. Application of technique is the same.

A *Pilot/Co-Pilot* assists a *Seeker* in *accessing* the *incidents* on the *Backtrack*. The *Pilot* is not particularly interested in the *significances* of the *energetic-masses* and *terminals* entangled there. That is more of an interest to the *Seeker* themselves, about their own case. But a *Pilot* needs to be interested in a *Seeker's* case, and help maintain the interest and *attention* level of the *Seeker* on their own case.

The easiest way to get started, is with whatever a *Seeker's attention* is currently on. It is common, at the beginning of a session, to ask: *"Has anything happened that's been a problem to you?"* Or, if you are able to *Pilot* a *Seeker* for multiple *sessions*, you might modify this with *"Since your last session...*" and so forth. This creates *communication-lines* and gets *attention* off of "*human problems*" — *domestics*, *money* or whatever, by simply *acknowledging* it.

When using a *GSR-Meter* (as described in "*Systemology Biofeedback*"): if there is a *high-resistance* (*balance-point*) at the start of the *session*, some preliminary PCL may be required to lower the *resistance-reading*. Examples of this would be:

"*Are you currently protesting something?*"

"*Has some condition gone on too long?*"

"*Has an achievement of yours not been acknowledged?*"

"*Are you having pains (body problems)?*"

"*Has something 'almost been found out'?*"

"*Is there something you can't tell anyone?*"

Even if not prompted to disclose/speak the information to the *Co-Pilot*, often just the *realization* of *attention being on* these things is enough to bring down the *resistance-reading*. Of course, this may require "*repeated spotting*" of the data "*As-It-Is*" to get the *balance-point* into "normal range." Once it is: the *Pilot* starts each *session* by *running* the "*preventative fundamentals.*"

THE PRELIMINARY INTERVIEW

Prior to any *processing*-regimen or standard *session*, the relationship between the *Pilot* and *Seeker* really begins with a *formal interview*. This allows the *Pilot* to get familiar with a *Seeker* and their *case*. But this is still best conducted in a *session-like* environment—and using a *GSR-Meter*.

The *Pilot* can ask the *Seeker* about times they've encountered trouble during their life—noting the *Meter-reads*, and the *area* or *terminal* that it *registers* on. This is only to determine the background and also to help steer what *areas/terminals* will require handling; but *processing* is not part of the *preliminary interview* itself.

The interview helps a *Pilot* "locate" areas with *fragmentary charge* prior to an actual *processing-session*; but also to gauge the *Seeker's attention* and *communication-lag*.

If a *Seeker* is experiencing *low-Awareness* states in-*session* —and/or they have no *reality* on any *recall-type processing* (*analytical recall*)—then focus on "*objective-style*" *processes* that involve *objects* and *masses* in their environment— even *points in space* if they can be worked up to it. This will provide a greater sense of *relief* for their present *state* than initially trying to go after the deeper sources of *turbulence*.

A key point of the interview is for a *Pilot* to get *reality* on a *Seeker's case*. You want to know what is the *Seeker's* ideal picture of *Life*, what is their existing situation, and how far of a departure is one from the other. By knowing this, we can bridge the gap in their *perceptions*—gradually separating the *Seeker's* "*Personal Universe*" from the "*Physical Universe*" in which it is entangled. A *true realization* of this *differentiation* is how one eventually "*Ascends.*"

There are many ways to engage in an interview—and a *Pilot* is likely to develop their own style for this as they gain more experience. You might simply say: "*Tell me about your life.*"

One popular interview technique is often referred to as the "*Spheres Assessment.*" In this practice: you simply go down the list of *Spheres of Existence*—and representative *terminals* for them—and note if there is a *Meter-read*, and/or there is noticeable *"charge"* based on the *Seeker's* observable reactions to each.

For the first *Sphere*, you have the *Body*, the *Human life*, their *name*, *&tc*. You move on to the second *Sphere*, concerning *"Home,"* and you have anything involving *domestic life*, or various *family-roles*, like *"mother"* or *"husband,"* *&tc*. And you just keep going through all of the facets of existence in this manner. By noting the reactions to the various *areas* and *terminals*, a *Pilot* can apply *processing-levels 0-to-6* more effectively for a *Seeker*; targeting specific areas of *turbulence* that are holding them down.

A *Pilot* wants to pay particular attention to *Spheres* three (*groups*), seven (*spirits*) and eight (*divinity* and *religion*). You want to know what spiritual, mystical, social, philosophical, or religious groups and practices the *Seeker* has been involved with prior to *Systemology*. There is likely to be a lot of *imprinting* for these areas.

The obvious area to target is whatever a *Seeker* is most "upset" about (in present-time). Locate the *"can't do" justifications* or *considerations* attached to that.

Goals or *Purposes* are also heavily charged areas—which we treat more directly in *AT#2* and *PC-12*. But from the beginning, a *Pilot* should know what a *Seeker* wants to achieve in their life—their motivations and perceived purposes; but also *"failed goals"* and *"incomplete cycles-of-action."* By this, we mean, when they set out to do something, or intended something, but for whatever reason it didn't happen. It is likely some *Awareness* still remains on it.

THE SKILLS OF PILOTING

As said previously: *communication* is *level zero* for both the *Pathway* and *Pilot Training*. It is *step-one* of having a *session*. And it is key to everything else that we handle with our *Systemology*. Consider how far a *Seeker* could really get beyond *level-zero*, without the *ability* and *willingness* to *communicate* and *engage* on *any* subject; and without reactively *avoiding* what is *unpleasant* or *undesirable*.

Now, as we move into *Level-1*—"*handling problems*"—the first part, *communication*, already has to be in place; established. It is on such an incremental or gradual incline that we *ascend* the *Pathway*. Stable progress is built upon the foundations of previous stabilized progress. This is the only way that one can be sure of their own progress; and that nothing has been accepted blindly—or "*on faith*," as is said.

Most *session*-difficulties—whether *Solo* or *Co-Piloted*—generally stem from one of the *preventative fundamentals*. So, when in question, this should be checked periodically throughout a *session*, to make sure they don't require additional attention; or that something hasn't happened *in-session* (such as the *Pilot* making a mistake) that has put the *Seeker out-of-session*.

If a *Seeker* seems suddenly put-off by the *Pilot* or the *session*, the correct question to ask is: "*What have I done wrong?*" You do not ask "*if you did something wrong*," because a *Seeker* is likely to just say "*no*," or be dismissive. The *Seeker* may still indicate that you did nothing wrong; but by asking in this way, you also have a chance to check for any reaction on the *Meter*. It also gives them a better chance to volunteer information; because you *do* really want to know. A *Seeker* going *out-of-session* is easily missed; then you wonder why they aren't making further progress.

A *Pilot* needs to have an understanding of *two-way communication* and skill in its use. This is not only important for *processing*, but also for understanding the relay of information that occurs internally between systems; for example, following the *ZU-Line* from the *Alpha-Spirit* through *mental circuitry* and finally engaging with a *body*. All of these components are in *communication* with one another — usually *fragmented*, but it is still *communication*.

A *Pilot* should also understand the *Beta Awareness Scale*. This helps you determine what level a *Seeker* is *communicating from*. For example: an *enthusiastic* person is going to *communicate* far differently than an *angry* person, or a *bored* person, *&tc*. Not only do they relay *communication* differently in their speech and behaviors, but they also will receive *communication* differently. For example: a *sad* person is not going to respond very well to someone coming at them *enthusiastically hyper, &tc*.

The other frequently missed-point is the handling of a *presently perceived problem*. This cannot be overstated; because there is some strange expectancy that *Systemology* will still produce stable results even if one's conscious *attention* is *fixedly* elsewhere; and it won't. Of course there is a lot of *fragmented Awareness* that is still suspended elsewhere; but what chance have we of reclaiming *that* if we can't pull together what *attention-units* we currently *are* in a position to *knowingly control*?

A *Pilot* should observe where a *Seeker's attention* is *fixed* on something that they perceive to be still in need of "solving" or "controlling"—*stopping, changing, &tc.*

A bit of our *Awareness* remains on a line to those *terminals* and *areas* that we are considering "*problems*," but of which are not actually present in our environment; only our personal or "mental" environment. And often, *"problems" are* generated compulsively and automatically by various *machinery, just to be* a "*problem*" for us—manufactured *just* to keep our *attention fixed on* all this nonsense; so we don't have a chance to figure out what is really going on. It's all been *systematically engineered* to operate that way; as becomes even more apparent in *upper-level* work.

A *Seeker* will get a handle on "*human problems*" after they get a certainty on being able to *create* them at will. Sounds a bit backwards, doesn't it; but it is truth. As long as an individual remains unable to *create* and *destroy* their own *machinery* and *circuitry*, they will remain *compulsively*—and often quite *unknowingly*—dependent on *programmed automation* to manufacture *reality* for them; based on long-forgotten and horribly *fragmentary reality-agreements* and *postulates*. In other words: they will remain ever "*at effect*."

Rather than *avoiding* areas, you want the *Seeker* to "*describe the problem*." You want to bring it into view, rather than having it linger perpetually on the periphery or side-view. Ask the *Seeker* if the problem seems "*farther away*" after each time they describe it. Our first goal here is to keep the solidity of *mental imagery* and entangled energy of the perceived problem from being right there up on the *Seeker* and overwhelming them. Because no real progress occurs that way. It has to be brought up—*resur-*

faced—and treated *analytically*; not remain down in *low-Awareness* levels of misemotion and such.

Another critical component to *processing*, and too often missed, is the *acknowledgment*. This is how a *Pilot* "ends" one cycle of action, or communication, or in most cases, a single PCL. *"Thank You." "Okay." "Good."* It is an indication to the *Seeker* that their response has been received.

The *acknowledgment* is also important to keep the *Pilot* in check and following the standard procedures. Each PCL is given in its own unit of time and is a complete cycle of action. It isn't just one long string of commands.

Once a PCL is complete, the *Pilot acknowledges* its completion or response given. Then, when the *Pilot* speaks again, they are starting a *new* cycle-of-action or communication; they are *not* leading off of the *Seeker's* previous response. This is the only way to maintain *control* of a *session*. Let me tell you how to quickly lose *control* of a *session*. You ask a *Seeker*, *"How are you?"* And they say, *"Not well."* And you say, *"Oh, how come?"* bzzzt—crash! You've just lost *control* of the *session*.

You've got to maintain *communication* without treating a *session* like two buddies having a good-ol' conversation. That is really not what *systematic processing* is. And you won't make any solid gains that way. You say *"Okay, thank you for telling me"* so they don't feel ignored. But if you keep letting a *fragmented Seeker* "steer the ship" than you aren't a very good *Pilot*. The *acknowledgment* also ensures that a *Seeker's attention* does not remain *fixed* on any incomplete cycles-of-action due to the *session* itself. There are such things as *session repair-actions*; where a *Seeker* must essentially *repair* a *processing*-mistake that can occur whether *Solo* or *Co-Piloted*.

To *repair* a *processing-error*, a *Seeker* simply "*Spots*" the point where it occurred and then handles it properly. In the case of a *Piloting* error: the *Seeker* would "*Spot*" it and respond; and the *Pilot acknowledges* that response. For example: they "*Spot*" when you were shuffling papers around and it bothered them. You just say, "*Okay, thank you*" and "*is it alright with you if we continue the session?*" You're back in business. You don't need to get bogged down in blame. Just keep the *session* going.

The last point that I want to make—and it seems strange that we should need to point this out—but: *processing* is about the *Seeker*. The *Seeker* is the focus.

Going back to what is said about *sessions* not being a "simple conversation": there is sometimes a tendency for *Pilots* to do too much of the *talking*. Having studied the subject of *Systemology* more intensely, they generally know a great deal about what is happening with a *Seeker* that the *Seeker* hasn't fully *recognized* or *realized* yet for themselves. Don't deny your *Seekers* a chance to achieve these *realizations* for themselves; given them their *wins*.

But the point is: its the *Seeker's* time. This isn't a time for the *Pilot* to bring up their own case or editorialize the *Seeker's*. Your own stuff is for your *sessions*, when you are getting *processing*. Let's not have any of that "*Oh, yeah, this one time I...*" If you want to share stories of the *Backtrack*, save it for discussions that are not *in-session*.

The initial interview is also *two-way communication*—but the focus is still entirely on the *Seeker's* case; not yours. You don't want to be doing all the talking; that isn't going to make the *Seeker* get any better. You do enough *talking* to keep the *Seeker* engaged and attentive. Some good example questions to keep them *focused*, include:

"What are you interested in?"

"What activities do you enjoy?"

"What makes you happy?"

"What have you been successful at?"

"What do you feel you must do? —must not do?"

"Tell me about it."

"What do you think that is about?"

"How have you dealt with that?"

"Who else was involved?"

Whatever technique or application of our *Systemology* is handled by a *Pilot* or *Minister*, the stable results will only occur by handling the *Alpha-Thought*—the underlying continuously created or generated *postulates*, *considerations*, and *reality-agreements*, that are keeping the *Seeker's attention-Awareness* suspended on an *entangled fragmentary existence*, rather than actually *confronting reality* and treating it *"As-It-Is."* Once a *Seeker* has reached that point, a *Pilot* can step back and let the *Seeker fly!*

For the first time ever in history: we have the *Map*; we have the *spiritual technology*; and we have the *training* available. So, let's work together now, and start helping one another get out of this mess. Let's help one another reach *Ascension!*

SYSTEMOLOGY
PROCEDURES
MANUAL

SYSTEMATIC PROCESSING & THE ALPHA-SPIRIT

Fragmentation occurs due to our desire to *create* (or *copy*) and *experience "everything."* In our native state, as a *god-like being*, this amounts to little more than watching a thrilling movie every once and a while to keep some of the more desirable conditions of existence *'fresh'*. We are, after all, quite *eternal*, and *boredom* is always a *fear*. But, this does not mean that the *effects* of these *creations* must *persist* and go on to perpetuate as *fragmentation* thereafter.

Actualized individuals are able to shake off *effects* of *fragmentation* like water. This is what a *Seeker* is improving on the *Pathway*. The existence—and our continuous *unknowing creation*—of *fragmentation* is a quite unfortunate mistake we all have picked up quite early on our *Spiritual Timeline* and tracked along with us ever since.

Spiritual implanting (taking place long before the existence of *this Physical Universe*) misled us to believing that *thinking about, perceiving, experiencing* and/or *creating* certain "things" could actually permanently harm us. This resulted in us *"flinching"* or *"withdrawing"* from "things" for the very first time. Later, those same things were used to discourage and restrict our *thinking about, looking at, doing* and even *being* things—and now, we have found our *spiritual perception* quite *darkened*, and our *spiritual abilities* quite *fragmented*.

We exist as a *Potential Everythingness* that is balancing an *Infinity-of-Nothingness*; we never seem to allow ourselves to be rid of anything unless we have a *certainty* that we can *create* (*have*) it again in the future.

To *"lose"* anything permanently—even if only a *created mental image picture*—would be to take away (or reduce) the full quality of richness inherent in *Everythingness*.

This also means that an individual will not '*uncreate*' any of their *continuously created* "things" unless they can *look at* a "thing" so clearly and completely *"As-It-Is,"* that they could *create* (*have*) it again.

The 'things' of *fragmentation unknowingly persist* because we believe that we should not *look at* them, and certainly not *create* them *knowingly* so as to have *responsibility* for their *creation*. When we *create* "mental image" *facsimile-copies* in our *processing exercises*, we demonstrate to an individual that they are capable of *recreating* at *will*. When we treat the *copy "As-It-Is,"* we also demonstrate they have abilities to make it "go away" or "disappear" too. Hence, when we bring something up "into view" during *systematic processing*, we are, at the very least, able to '*desensitize*' some of the *fragmentation effects* using our *Awareness*.

The *willingness* to *create* something is also governed by the *willingness* to be *responsible* for the existence of a thing —and the effects that it *creates*. True *power* and *control* is only found in *full responsibility*. It also requires having *clear communication* and *perception*. These are all areas that a *Seeker* will target and improve upon with *systematic processing* on the *Pathway*.

Another part of *processing* is *"loosening of fixed considerations."* We are "reactively" inclined to not *like* 'things' that are "bad" —or two things in "conflict" with one another. We may even think "changing our mind" about a thing is a betrayal. Yet to be rid of any "bad" conditions, we must first decide to *"like"* it enough to *confront* it *"As-It-Is."* We must be able to at least *tolerate* it enough, have it *close* enough (for our *perception*), even for a moment, in order to *look at* it. We don't have to *have* it again; but we must be *willing* to *recreate* it in order for it to truly cease to *persist*.

Our methods represent the *systematic* opposite of how things are handled in a "human society" where things are continuously *suppressed* and buried out of view — which makes certain that the *fragmentation* goes on being *compulsively created unknowingly* out of our *control*.

Procedures and techniques for *systematic defragmentation* require skill and practice to be effective. The *"Pathway to Ascension" Professional Course* was designed with the *"Solo-Pilot"* in mind — though our original *Systemology Core* volumes (collecting the research and development) emphasized what is now called *"Traditional Piloting"* (where a trained professional "guides" a *Seeker* along the *Pathway*).

"Traditional Piloting" is not an option for *Systemology Level-7* and above. Even if a *Seeker* is *"Co-Piloted"* through earlier *processing-levels*: to continue with *"Advanced Training"* requires they study the *"Professional Course"* on their own — in addition to these *"Advanced Training Supplements"* — before using the *"Keys to the Kingdom" Advanced Training Course* as a *Solo-Pilot*.

Ideally, a *Seeker* will learn skills and gain the *certainty* necessary to apply *systematic processing* "as" *Self*, "to" *Self*. In the end, this is the only truly workable and effective method of *"setting one's Self free."*

A *"free being"* that is not bound to a *Body* must also not be entirely reliant on *"biofeedback devices"* in order to maintain their *freedom* later on. However, to ensure we get there (relatively quickly)—and to learn how it is even possible—"*biofeedback technology*" is a critical tool applied to some *upper-level* procedures found in the "*Advanced Training Course.*" Basic details are given in the "*Systemology Biofeedback*" *Advanced Training Supplement*. Additional details are given in various course books.

The theory behind our approach is that: what an individual *actually knows* and/or is *knowingly creating*, is not the source of their *fragmentation*. But, in our present condition, if we *could* intuitively and instinctively *defragment* ourselves without the right training and use of technology, then we would have been "*out of here*" already. Of course, we've swallowed a lot of *false data* early in our existence, and this set the foundations—and *platforms*—for our being *fragmented*. Unfortunately, this is what causes our "*instinct*" to often lead us away from the upward *Pathway*.

A *Biofeedback* "*device*" is not described in the "*Professional Course*" materials, so that a *Seeker does* get practice handling our methods "*intuitively*" without it. This experience could be applied to *upper-levels*, approaching them without a "*device*," but the progress is likely to be much slower.

SYSTEMATIC PROCEDURES

Systematic Processing is primarily *looking* and *seeing* "*What Is*"—*As-It-Is*. "*Processing Command Lines*" (or "*PCL*") are really a query-line (or question) of "*what is*"? The response is based on whatever our *attention* (*Awareness*) is on, or directed to. Even when not worded as a literal question, a PCL is still a prompt for such a response. For example:

Q: *Recall a time when... (What is it?)*
A: *(It is) when such-and-such...*

Q: *Spot something in the... (What is it?)*
A: *(It is) that thing...*

Q: *Notice something about... (What is it?)*
A: *(It is) this...*

A *Seeker* is still permitted to *consider* or *wonder about* things. But to avoid having progress slow down to a halt during a *processing session*: the focus should be on what they *can identify, see,* or *know about,* rather than concentrating on *"unknowns."* We can *consider* things we do not yet have a *Knowingness* of, but usually the solution is to work from a stable point, which rests on what we *do know* with *actual certainty.*

Systematic Processing also involves *"spotting" What-Is "repeatedly."* The best gains in *perception* occur when something is first *looked at.* Just watching it thereafter does not produce nearly as much change in *perception* for the amount of time spent doing so. Therefore, *attention* is often alternated "on" and "off" of something in order to *see* it more *clearly.* Or, you can shift *attention* onto different parts of large objects or a significant *"incident"* (rather than simply "stare" at it).

Some basic *processes* practice intentionally *reaching* and *withdrawing*; on a "physical" level, and with *attention.* When an area is *fragmented,* a *Seeker's attention* is either fixedly "stuck" *on* it, or else they have a "mental flinch" *away* from it (and are unlikely to *look* at all). To *defragment,* we *systematically* put *attention* "onto" and "off" of it

—*knowingly* and *intentionally*—in order to restore ability to clearly and *Self-Honestly* think about and/or handle something.

There are times an individual might get away with applying *"fixed concentration"* to something—but it is usually the "long way" to get results. There is also a tendency to build up an "energetic resistance" when something is "pushed" against for too long. Rather than swing a hammer once and just keep pressing hard against a nail, we get better results by *alternating* our *efforts* with *repetitive* swings.

To be effective, *systematic processing* is applied to only one thing/area at a time. It is for this reason that a *Pilot* must be aware of where a *Seeker's attention* is *fixed*—or a *Solo-Pilot* must be aware of it. If it *is* "stuck" on a point that can't be put aside enough to do something else, then it must be addressed first in *processing*, because that is the *fixed* point of *attention* that all other *processing* will take place from anyways. The *"presence"* that is elsewhere must be brought under *control* before other gains will be made *"in-session."*

There are some procedures we present as *processing*, but which are really *"exercises"* that may not have a specific *"end-point"*— for example: practicing a skill or ability with *"repetitive doing."* These are often referred to as *"objective processes"* since they pertain to the *"external environment,"* even when practiced mentally—such as: *"Spot three points outside the building"* (which is alternated with *"three points in the room"*).

Most general *processes*, which get a *Seeker* to *confront* things, are *"repetitive"* in style. The goal is to push *through* something—some perceived *barrier*—or else "*un-*

cover" something to reveal *deeper* and *deeper* layers, until you can "*spot*" a basic "*answer*" (or "*confront*" an underlying "*incident*"), at which, the 'area' becomes *defragmented*.

A more specific type of *process* might require going through a "prepared list" of "items" (*terminals* or *areas*) to see which is the most "turbulent" or "reactive." For example: terminals for the "*Spheres of Existence*" might be listed ("*Self*," "*Home*," "*Family*," "*Groups*," &tc.) and the goal is to find the *most correct answer*. It may be that the *Seeker* is already *knowingly aware* of the "*answer*." But a more "*systematic*" approach is to apply *Biofeedback* (*e.g. GSR-Meter*) and see what "reacts" (or gives the largest "*read*" on the *device*).

GSR-devices may also indicate sources of underlying *fragmentation* that the *Seeker* is not already aware of. But, it is important not to treat the *device* itself as some kind of "*oracle*." It simply allows a *Pilot* to *see* "*reactive-responses*" with electronic precision—not altogether different than the instruments used for *piloting an aircraft*.

Another underlying fundamental to our *systematic processing* involves having a *Seeker* do *knowingly* what they are already doing on *automatic* (or as an *automatic response*). This helps *Seekers* practice regaining full conscious *control*. On the surface, to an outsider, some might argue that elements of *hypnotism* are present here; and they would be half right. We are actually doing the *reverse* of *hypnotism*; and the "duplication" of the "automation" is also only one part of the procedure.

When working to regain *control* of something *operating* on *automatic*, the *Seeker* is already starting from a *hypnotic-like* point of *fixation* and *unknowingness*. It is, after all, their own *creations, copies* and *mechanisms* that are still *persisting* and *operating automatically.*

Only when a *Seeker* is *certain* that they have full *control* of "*doing*" or "*creating*" something *knowingly* "at will," can they give up the "hold" on the *automation* and not feel a sense of "loss."

If you *suppress* what is happening on *automatic*, a *Seeker* won't "let go" of it and it may get buried deeper. Then you end up with a *persistence* of both the *suppression* and the *automation* to handle.

The second part of this procedure is for a *Seeker* to alternately increase and decrease the *automated action*, rather than putting all *attention* forcefully on "stopping." In this wise, you would repeatedly alternate exaggerating the condition "worse," and then making it "better," until you can *systematically* regain full *control*.

"*Creativeness Processing*" involves practice with *creating mental imagery*. Our underlying *spiritual ability* (and native function) is "*To Create*." Some interestingly effective *processes* simply require a *Seeker* to *knowingly* "*create*" things under their *control*. If you *create* something *causatively*, then you don't have to *compulsively (on automatic)*.

For example: if *obsessively* worried about something, or there is a "*stuck picture*" (or "*imprint*"), then a *Seeker knowingly/intentionally* "*creates*" (or "*Imagines*") many "*copies*" (and alterations thereof) until the *mental imagery* is fully under their *control* (and no longer *reactive/persistent*).

Not only does the *persistent condition* get lessened; the ability to *confront* "it" (or the situation), increases. Withdrawing from it has a tendency to "pull in" or "manifest" more of what we don't want. By demonstrating a *willingness* to *create it*, there is an "out-flow" of energy in that area and no perceived "deficiency" or "loss" to be filled by unwanted/undesirable *creations*.

This procedure is only effective if a *Seeker* does *not* attempt to change (or alter) the actual "reactive" (or *imprinted*) *mental image* directly. This method requires one's own *conscious creation*; not an automatically generated *imprint* or "*old picture.*"

To be *certain* of this: a *Seeker* should make/*create* many "*copies*"; not just one. The *copies* may then be altered — their color, size, location, *&tc.* may be changed — in whatever ways are necessary for a *Seeker* to be certain that these "images" are *their own creation* and fully under *their own control*.

Full *responsibility* and *control* of *creation* also requires a *willingness* to handle the other side of it: *destruction* or "*uncreation.*" *Fragmentation* in this area alone is enough to hinder *creative ability*.

Of course, when one *knows* they can *recreate* at *will*, there is no reason to restrict *freedom* with a *persistence*. Our "stuck" (or "fixed") *attention-units* (*Awareness*) serve us much better when "*free*" and under our own total *conscious control* once again.

Although it is usually not problematic in *processes*, "*Create*" and "*Destroy*" are both "*hot buttons*" that have a potential to trigger (or *restimulate*) *turbulent fragmentation*. At *upper-levels*, we know this is because both are *keywords* (or *buttons*) used for "*spiritual implant platforms.*" Each of us is likely to have *some charge* on these words.

As a general rule for any procedure used:

Once a process starts to run, continue it until it is done.

While a *process* is *run*, other things often come into view, and there is a tendency to start chasing after those things rather than completing the original *process*. If something does come up: make a note of it to handle later in a separate *process*, and continue what you're doing. Otherwise, no *processing* will actually happen; you will just be following one "thought-trail" after another, rather than *processing* them.

The *"Pathway to Ascension" Professional Course* material demonstrates to a *Seeker* how to apply all of these *systematic procedures* to specific areas of their life. Getting "started" *in-session* is covered in the *Basic Course, Lesson-6, "Systemology Processing."* The real issue that we want to discuss here is: knowing when to "stop."

End-points of a *process* (and/or *session*) are when there is a "win"—a point of "gain" or "improvement." It may not be the total *"end-realization"* of a *"level,"* or some huge "breakthrough" every time; but in order to keep making stable progress: you need to *acknowledge the wins* as they happen.

It's a mistake to "push" too hard and too long on a *process*, hoping to achieve some "major advancement" meanwhile *invalidating* the actual *wins* along the way that may have gone unnoticed. Because they weren't *acknowledged* as such, the *process* ran "past" or "over" the point that one should have stopped. Once that layer of *realization* or *defragmentation* is established (assuming things still feel incomplete), then you continue in a later *process* or *session*, working from those stable gains.

The *"eureka"* or *"this is it!"* moments are critical to *acknowledge* along the way in order to establish the stability and certainty. *Invalidating*, or blowing past, these moments will interfere with further progress. We *"chisel"* away at an area of *fragmentation* until that critical point when it simply "cracks" and falls away. There is no absolute determination about which *process* (or for "how long") it will take for this to occur. But in order for it to occur, successful *chiseling* must be *acknowledged* as *actually happening*—as *reality*.

Defragmentation is a gradual process of relieving the "weight" off of the *Spirit*. This "weight" is mostly *persistently created entangled energy-masses*. A proper *"session"* should provide *some sense of release* to a *Seeker* for it to be effective. If a *process* is not *run long enough*, there is a general feeling of "incompleteness." A *Seeker* may feel irritable as a result. When first learning, *Solo-Pilots* often don't *run* a *process* long enough. This is why good record-keeping (or *"Flight-Logs"*) are important. Because, if this is determined to be the case, the simple solution is to spot the incomplete *process* and finish it. Irritability and hopeless feelings are good indicators for a *process* being *"under-run."*

The other side of this—*"over-run"*—tends to make things more *"solid"* or feel *"heavier."* Usually an area or target item was *defragmented* (a *release-point* was achieved) but since the *process* continues to target it as *being there*, it gets "pulled in" again, or else is *recreated*. This happens when a beginner expects a single *process* to handle everything, or do it all, when it really requires applying many different *processes*, each providing another step forward as a fairly quick progression.

Solo-Pilots are encouraged to go through the material of the *Professional Course* in a swift manner, with the expectation that the *Seeker* will make multiple passes over certain areas, rather than lingering on one *process* or *procedure* too long.

The *systematic* solution to an *"over-run" process* is to simply *"spot"* and *acknowledge* the point when the *"win"* or *"new realization"* had occurred (but was overlooked, not *acknowledged*, and *invalidated*).

PREVENTATIVE FUNDAMENTALS

If a *Seeker* has an *upset*, a *problem*, or any *attention* "stuck" on things they are worried about, it is not possible to progress in other areas until this handled. In the *Professional Course*, this handling is called "preventative fundamentals" because a *Pilot* must take care of these things first before attempting to spend *session* time in other areas. What we are *preventing* is an *invalidation* of our methods by a *Seeker* that is unable to apply *presence* of *attention in-session*. These fundamentals are treated in *Professional Course* materials:

1. A *break* or *upset* in the *"Flow-Factors"* — enforced or inhibited *communication, likingness* and/or *agreement*. [*PC Lesson-7, "Eliminating Barriers"*]

2. A *"Human Problem"* — present-time *attention* (*presence*) is occupied fixedly elsewhere (and outside one's own control). [*PC Lesson-4, "Handling Humanity"*]

3. A *"Hold-Out"* — *attention* restimulated an area, usually because someone else *almost found out* about it. [*PC Lesson-6, "Escaping Spirit-Traps"*]

A *Solo-Pilot* looks over this list and determines if any of these factors are in play at the start of a *session*. In *Traditional Piloting*, a *GSR-Meter* may be used to *assess* if anything on the list *reads*. For example:

1. "Is there a *break* or *upset* of a *Flow-Factor?*"

[if it *"reads,"* check]

   a. "Is there a break in *Communication?*"

   b. "On *Likingness?*"

   c. "On *Agreement?*"

[then, *run* on what *"reads"*]

   a. "Was this ___ *Enforced?*"

   b. *"Inhibited?"*

In this first case: when you can *spot* the primary underlying source of the *upset*—such as *"inhibited communication"* or *"enforced agreement"*—there should be *some* feeling of *"relief."* If not: you may need to *reassess* the list.

The *"relief on spotting"* is either partial or total. If total: *acknowledge* it and continue on with the *session*. If partial: handle the *upset* (or *flow-break*) before continuing. It is handled by *spotting* the *flow* and *circuit*.

For example: did *you inhibit (or enforce) someone else's communication (&tc.)* or did *someone else inhibit yours?* Perhaps it was observing *someone else inhibiting another*. Whatever the case: *identify it*, then *spot* exactly what *communication* was *inhibited*. Then *spot* yourself in the situation; what you *did* and *decided* as a result of it, *&tc*. If the *turbulence* doesn't resolve or worsens: look for an earlier incident that was similar. If it gets more *solid*, it has been *over-run*: *spot* the *release-point* that was missed.

PSYCHOSOMATICS & PAIN

Generally speaking: applying *systemology* to treat *"pain"* is an *advanced* practice. It is important to know that there will be a moment when the *pain* becomes sharper before it *releases*. This is because you have to remove a *mental barrier* that *suppresses* the *pain* in order to *confront it "As-It-Is."*

Such practices are not applied to *injury emergencies*—when other *"first aid"* is required for the *Body*; but they can greatly assist thereafter. Long-term use of *pain-suppression drugs* can interfere with abilities to handle *pain* with mental techniques.

The basic *"touch-back"* technique is given in the first *Professional Course (PC)* lesson. [See also *PC Lesson-5, 9* and *10.*] Although physical injury includes "loss" or "damage" to *cells*, the *pain*-sensation generated by the *"reactive control-center"* of the *Mind* is generally perceived as more extreme than what it actually is or should be.

Some 90% (or more) of what you feel as *"pain"* is really due to a *mental accumulation* of *"past pains,"* rather than that actual present-time moment. It accumulates like *imprint-chains*; in this case, *mental images* or *impressions* of the *pain*. It was once believed that all this information was only *imprinted* as "engram memories" onto a living *cell*. At *upper-levels*, we realize that this is only one part of the whole situation.

The subject of *"Spiritual Machinery"* is introduced in *PC Lesson-14*. We have parts of our *Awareness* hidden away, *compulsively creating machinery*, much of which is intimately connected to the *Body*. This is why when the *Body* "stubs" *its toe*, you get a sense that *you* "stubbed" *your toe*. The *machinery* detects the physical action and generates the *pain*-sensation for you to experience as *reality*.

An individual can also get *restimulated* by the environment (or a particular thought) and trigger this *machinery* to generate a *pain*-sensation. Even if no physical impact occurred to cause it, the same *impression* is sensed as *real*; the same *machinery* has been activated as if an injury is present. Any *systematic procedure* for this would require getting more of that *machinery* under the *Seeker's conscious control*.

The *advanced technique* (*exercise*) for handling *pain, sensation, emotion*, or even *drug effects*, is to practice placing (*whatever it is*) into walls, floors, ceilings, or large objects in view. In this wise, we do not "stop" or "suppress" the *machinery*; we do not try to leave ourselves numb. We *redirect* the *flow* (with *intention/attention*) to locations *external* to the *Body*. We *confront it As-It-Is*, but while it's being directed "*over there.*" Most *Seekers* start by using a "*wall.*"

Much like other collected "experiences" or *creations* discussed in this manual: an individual won't be able to fully let go of something unless they are certain it can be *recreated* at *will*. This includes *sensations*; even undesirable ones. *Machinery* is a form of *automation*; so "procedures" for regaining *control* of it can apply here too.

Our *advanced technique* is not particularly *easy*—especially if being practiced for the first time during an extreme situation. The exercise should be practiced on *emotions* first; gaining greater *control* over *emotional machinery*, while also earning more experience with these procedures.

When first practicing, a *Seeker* may only get the vaguest sense or an *imagined* idea that there is a faint *sensation* in the "*wall.*" Just keep practicing with this. Also, don't concentrate too hard on just one particular point on the "*wall.*" This works best when briskly moving from spot to spot, alternating between spots, or simply going around the room. Use all six basic directions; not just the "*wall*" in front of you.

After a *Seeker* is successful employing this "*wall*"-technique with significant results, if additional handling is required, gradient steps for improving *machinery control* (directing it into the "*walls*" *&tc.*) are:

A. Alternate: *spots near* to and *far* from the *Body* (including *large objects*).

B. Alternate: *spots* in the *walls* and *spots* inside the *Body* (but not where the *pain* actually is).

C. Alternate: *spots* in the *walls* and *spots* inside the *Body* (where it actually is).

D. Alternate: *spots* where it is and *spots* where it isn't (inside the *Body*).

With the total sensation being moved *on* and *off* the *spot* in the *Body*, greater *control* should occur. This does not treat all of the underlying issues of, for example, what *imprints* and *postulates* may be activating various *machinery*. That still requires other *processing*; but if a *Seeker's attention* is mostly fixed on *pain*, then that condition must be handled first as a fundamental.

There is another *advanced technique* (that requires *Systemology Level-6* proficiency). It involves making many *facsimile-copies* of a sensation (preferably out to *infinity* as practiced with the *Professional Course*) on opposite sides of an injured or painful area; then pushing them into the

Body simultaneously; doing this many times from multiple axis/directions.

A *Seeker* makes certain to *alter* their *copies* to make sure they are *their creation*. Start with one pair of *copies* until you can make them in "batches" (and preferably out to *infinity*).

The trick is to stay determined. This isn't applied at *lower-levels* because of the *ability-to-confront* (*Awareness*) that is required. The chronic sensations come off in layers, *resurfacing* each similar occurrence for this particular *Body* until the first injury or *pain*-incident is contacted.

The *perception* of *sensation* can shift fairly quickly; but you continue until it feels like you've hit the basic one. When that one falls away and you feel better, you *end* the *process*. *Running* it even one PCL longer may pull in sensations for that area from an earlier *Body* you once used.

This technique can also be practiced with making *copies* of entire areas of the *Body*, not just the sensation itself. Another trick to it is that when one layer of sensation (or incident) falls away, you *acknowledge* it and switch *attention* to the same area on the other side of the *Body*, repeating the same with *copies* of whatever is there. If there is no sensation felt there, just *copy* the physical structure (area) that *is* there. Then you can switch back to the original side you were treating (if layers remain).

SPIRITUAL IMPLANTS & ENTITIES

In *PC Lesson-11*, we introduce "*Spiritual Implants.*" Handling these *heavy conditioning incidents* (and their *effects*) is a significant part of *Systemology Level-7* and above. The subject of *Entities* is treated at *Level-8*.

In *this Physical Universe, Implants* are laid in by *force* and *electronic waves*. In earlier *Universes*, before *Alpha-Spirits* considered they could be hurt, *Implanting* included using *aesthetic waves, emotion* and *symbols* to embed/encode *false information*.

Implants consist of a *systematic sequence* of *considerations* or *postulates* (*Alpha Thought*) that are intentionally "*charged/fragmented*" in order to *control* an individual's *reality*. We *process-out* these thought-intentions as "*command-items*." They are not our original thoughts, but they are reinforced with a *charge* as if they *are* our own intentions.

Implants often contain a repeating *pattern* of opposing "*items*." Some *Implants* are more complex, using repeating *patterns* within other *patterns* on a declining scale. We refer to a single *sequence* of the complete *pattern* as an "*Implant Platform*." It provides a "*plane*," "*surface*" or "*filter*" for an area, which affects later *fragmentation*.

An *Implant Platform* may contain over *100* "*command-items*"—each of which requires *defragmentation* in *sequence*. For this reason, standard procedures at *advanced levels* utilize a *Biofeedback Device*. A *Platform* list is *processed-out* by repeatedly "*spotting*" a "*command-item*" until it ceases to *read* on a *GSR-Meter*; then, going to the next *item* and doing the same.

Some basic techniques for *defragmenting Implants*" are given in *PC Lesson-11*. For *Level-5*, without a *GSR-Meter*, the most basic procedure is:

A. *"Spot (or Imagine) an implant-item (or command-item in the listed sequence)."*

B. *"Confront it until it ceases to have any effect."*

The easiest way for a *Seeker* to accomplish this is to alternately:

A. *"Spot the implanted command-item."*

B. *"Spot something in the room."*

"*Command-Items*" are/were not *implanted* in "English" (or any language of Human speech). Therefore, the best we can do for *processing* is to "*approximate*" their meaning (*get a sense* for their original *intention*) when each "*command-item*" is "*Spotted.*"

When a *GSR-Meter* is applied to this practice, then "*Step-B*" is technically replaced with "*Spotting the Meter display for reads.*"

A *Seeker* "*Spots*" the "*item*" and then immediately checks the *Meter* for a "*read.*" It is best if the *list* and the *Meter* are next to each other, in easy view. This continues, alternating *attention* between the "item" and the *Meter* until no "*charge*" is *reading.*

Simply reading through an *item-list* is not sufficient to *process-out* the *significances*. Just staring at an *item* doesn't do much good either. *Attention* shifts "*on*" and "*off*" an *item* is what is required. Some reasons for this are explained previously in this manual. In some cases it may be beneficial to *alternate* between *two* directly "opposing" *items*; also called a "*pair.*" And when that *pair* is *defragmented*, you go to the next *pair*. But not all *Implant-Platforms* are designed with *item-pairs*.

Implant-handling is always *Piloted Solo*. If a *Seeker* runs into excessive *turbulence* doing so, a *systematic* solution is to *spot* the beginning of the *Implant* or *incident*. That means the first *item* on the list; or even the events of the *incident* leading up to the *Implant*. It is for this reason that the *"Entry-Into-This-Universe"* (or *Heaven Implant*) is the first one that a *Seeker* is introduced to (*PC Lesson-11*). Being the first one used for *this Physical Universe*, it may be *spotted* to relieve some *pressure* off of more recent *Implant-Platforms* or *incidents*.

This specific *entry-incident* applies only to *this Physical Universe*. Each *Universe* has its own *Entry-Point Implant* to assign the *reality-parameters* of *that Universe*. Each *incident* makes an *impression* that *it* is the *"Beginning of Time,"* but it is really only the beginning of an *Alpha-Spirit's* experience within *that Universe*. Note that *spotting* such things does not *defragment* more recent *Implants*, but it is powerful enough to pull *attention* away from *restimulation* that working with *Implants* might trigger.

As a *false "Beginning of Time,"* each *entry-incident* also *Implants* a *false* "native state" for an *Alpha-Spirit*—meaning a *Beingness* or *"purpose"* impressed as an individual's own original and basic function. For example: in *this Physical Universe*, the basic game-goal is: *"To Survive."* This is laid in with an *Implanting-Incident* that also reinforces an idea that we must compete with each other to retain this "native state." Everything about the *Implant* is a "lie," but it sets up the *game* we experience in this version of *Beta-Existence*.

The earliest known *Implant-Series* appears to set up the structure for everything else. It is referred to as the *"Jewel of Knowledge"* and is treated at *Systemology Level-7*. An understanding of all these *Implants* is critical for handling *Entities* at *Level-8*. The purpose of an *Implant* is to get an *Alpha- Spirit* to *compulsively create* a *condition*, including the *Universe* they're experiencing.

The subjects of *Entities* is not introduced early on the *Pathway* for the same reason as *Spiritual Implants*. These areas require a *high-level Awareness* and *ability-to-confront*. It is also important for a *Seeker* to regain a certain degree of *Self-determination* and the ability to properly *identify* "*conditions*" and "*sources.*" Otherwise we will improperly assign all "*cause*" to *external* factors, and lose *responsibility* and *control* of handling our *fragmented creations*.

Entities have very little ability to affect us directly. They are *subtle facets* of our more *visible* environment with an equal ability to "trigger," *restimulate*, or otherwise remind us of unpleasant things. More details on handling *Entities* is given in the *Advanced Training Course* material for *Systemology Level-8*.

SOLO-PILOTING UPPER-LEVELS

Professional Pilots are trained at the *Mardukite Academy of Systemology* using the *Systemology Core Research Volumes*. While our new *Professional Course* sidesteps the requirement of a *Co-Pilot*, it does not replace all of the knowledge that goes with that role.

Our *Basic*, *Professional*, and *Advanced* materials are all expertly designed for the greatest effectiveness and conciseness. It does not, however, provide *all* of the information that is available on the various subjects. Since every student may not have time available to study all the background research, these *Advanced Supplements* have been prepared. However, if a *Solo-Pilot* still finds a certain area difficult to understand, they should refer to the *Systemology Core Research Volumes*.

Although *Solo-Piloting* does not carry the same two-person element as *Traditional Piloting*, the same rules apply to the *Processing Communication Cycle* (see "*Metahuman Destinations: Volume One*"), and particularly critical when treating *upper levels* and *Flying-Solo* with a *GSR-Meter*. *Upper-level* materials will provide instructions, "*processing command-lines*" ("PCL"), and/or "*command-items*" (for *Implants*). A *Solo-Pilot* must understand the *command* and *procedures* before *running* anything as a *process*.

The *Seeker* then concentrates and silently *intends* the PCL as a *communication* from *Self*-to-*Self*. If there is "*charge*" on it, then there is an *answer* or *response (reaction)*. By paying *attention* to this *answer*, there is an *acknowledgment*—and that *ends* one complete *communication cycle*.

Biofeedback Devices can play a role in *Solo-Piloting* to assist recognizing when *charge* on an *item* is present—even if "beneath the surface" and not otherwise noticed. When there is no longer a *meter-read*, that is *acknowledged* as an *end-cycle* for the PCL. Unlike *Traditional Piloting*, a *Solo-Pilot* will rarely employ spoken PCL. In fact, starting with *Systemology Level-5*, more of the *processing* operates purely on an *intention* or *Alpha-Thought* level. If using a *GSR-Meter*, a *Seeker* must be able to both read a PCL and keep an eye on a *meter* for *reads*.

It is important to catch the *first read* on an *item*, because some *items* may not give a second *read* immediately afterward. This is another reason we prefer to shift *attention* "*on*" and "*off*" an *item*. But unless a *Seeker* catches the *first read*, it may *invalidate* the remaining *process*. It is also helpful to practice the skill of *"seeing"* something as if for the *first time*.

If your model of *GSR-Meter* requires using *two electrodes* (*one* for each hand), then it has to be modified for *Solo-Piloting*. All that needs to be done is make it so both *electrodes* can be held in one hand, in order to properly operate the *Meter* knobs. In most cases, the two *electrodes* are like hollow metal *"cans"* that can be attached with a *spacer* or empty *paper-towel roll* (to keep the two *electrodes* from touching, or else *short-circuiting*).

There is another *advanced* matter in these areas that must also be addressed. When a *Seeker* has reached *upper-level processing*, their *Awareness* has improved; their ability to affect the *Mind* with *intention* and *Alpha-Thought* is much stronger. This also means they've developed an ability to *intentionally* affect *Meter-reads*.

During a *Solo-session*: if a PCL *reads*, but a *Seeker* knows they had instantly thought "NO!" as a response, you can easily just check (with the *Meter*) *"Did the PCL read on 'No'?"* It might *read* again, which will confirm this, so you *acknowledge* *"It read on 'No',"* and continue your *processing*.

SYSTEMOLOGY BIOFEEDBACK MANUAL

THE SYSTEMOLOGY OF GSR-BIOFEEDBACK
(A SUMMARY)

This manual is restricted to students using: *The Systemology Professional Course* and/or *The Advanced Training Course*. It is not a matter of secrecy, but rather, proper understanding. This manual is a supplement that *advances* other material given in the aforementioned lessons. Its intended meaning and usage is not likely to be *fully realized* without prior experience in our methods of *systematic processing*.

Biofeedback Systemology is only introduced to a *Seeker* after completing *Systemology Level-4* (of the *Professional Course* material) at minimum. It is better for a *Solo-Pilot* to have experience with all basic *processing* first *without* using any *Biofeedback devices*. These are used to *"clear up"* lower-level "residual," but mainly for *advanced* work.

Traditional Piloting often includes some *Biofeedback metering device* as a tool for increasing a *Pilot's* ability to clearly indicate a *Seeker's* areas of *fragmentation* during *processing*. In this wise, such *devices* might effectively apply to *all processing-levels*.

| For *Solo-Pilots*, the most significant applications for *Biofeedback devices* pertain to *Systemology Level-5* and above (through the *Advanced Training Levels*). |

Let us begin with a quick summary of the most applicable basics. The remainder of this manual will cover more information in detail.

During the early development and practice of *"psychotherapy,"* Carl Jung realized that measurable *"electrical res-*

istance" in the *Human Body* responded automatically to *"mental reactions"* (regarding, for example, specific *questions* or *words*). This is called *"galvanic skin response"* (or "GSR"), because this response is detected with a *"galvanometer"* —or *"Ohm-meter."*

GSR technology may be used to detect changes in the *"electrical resistance"* on the surface of the skin. But these changes are so small that a standard *"ohmmeter"* (as an electrician might use) is not functional for our purposes. The total "range" that a standard meter covers on its dial is too large—and usually has no adjustment for "sensitivity" or other "calibration."

Jung's early research led to two main applications: one being integrated into traditional *"polygraph"* equipment (which is to say, the *"lie detector"*); and the other being developed for *spiritual defragmentation* practices and *"mental health"* studies. Including *Jung*, it has a long history of usage among *New Thought* practitioners.

In physics, *electrical resistance* is measured in *"ohms."* When *fragmentation* is not in *restimulation*, the *Human Body* generally registers between *5,000* and *12,500 ohms.* This is an ideal range to be within at the start of a session for *Advanced Processing.*

Just as additional *"mass"* or *"matter"* can more greatly *"block," "restrict,"* or *"resist"* a *current* or *flow*, so too with *"resistance"* on an *"electrical circuit."* The greater the *"mental mass"* in *restimulation*, the greater the *electrical resistance* "read" on a *meter*.

A *"meter read"* of *25,000* to *60,000 ohms* might indicate the presence of *"charged fragmentation"* presently active (or *restimulated*) in a *Seeker's "Personal Universe"* —and this impinges on, or *affects*, the *Human Body* in detectable ways. A sudden "surge" up into this area can also occur when a *process* has been *"overrun"* (used past the point of *defragmentation* or when whatever was targeted got handled). This is usually remedied by "*Spotting*" the moment the actual "*relief*" or "*release*" point had occurred and *recognizing* it as such.

Visible *reactions* displayed by a *GSR-Meter* "*needle*" reflect the moment-to-moment *reactions* occurring with a *Seeker* during *processing*. This is important for exploring the "*almost knowns*" that remain "out-of-sight," but are *accessible*.

Biofeedback meters do not "read" (*react*) on *data* that is still "deeply buried" (and/or which a *Seeker* has *no* present-time "*reality*" on). *Systematic Processing* is intended to "uncover" what is only "partially hidden" in order to bring more "deeply hidden" data into a range accessibility. The "reads" for "*almost knowns*" are instantaneous, because a *Seeker* isn't using "*mental circuitry*" to *think* about these *things*; any *energetic-charge* detected in this range is purely *reactive*.

Several *GSR-Biofeedback* applications are mentioned within previous course materials and volumes of the *Systemology Core*. It does, however, require having not only the *equipment*, but also an *understanding* and practical *experience*, for any effective use. This manual can only help provide the *understanding*, leaving the other components for a *Seeker* to acquire.

Some of our research to support application of *GSR-Biofeedback* to *systematic processing* included:

Jung, Carl: "*Studies in Word Analysis*"
Mathison, Volney: "*Manual of Electropsychometry*" (1951)

Mathison, Volney: "*Super-Visualization: The Duplicative Techniques of Applied Creative Energy*" (1956)

Gallert, Mark: "*Electropsychometry: A New, More Effective and Faster Psychotherapy*" (1955)

Shepherd, Peter: "*GSR-Meter Course: Biofeedback Monitoring Skills in the Context of Transformational Psychotherapy*"

Khazan, Inna: "*Biofeedback & Mindfulness in Everyday Life: Practical Solutions for Improving Your Health & Performance*"

Apter, Michael: "*Reversal Theory*" and "*Personality Dynamics*"

Gerbode, Frank: "*Beyond Psychology: Traumatic Incident Reduction*"

THE HISTORY & DEVELOPMENT OF GSR-BIOFEEDBACK METERING

Experimental use of "*Psycho-Galvanometers*" (or *GSR-Meters*) for "transpersonal psychology" is as old as "psychology" and "psychoanalysis" itself. That the surface of skin is *electrically conductive*—and that *detectable resistance changes* occur from *emotional stimulation*—dates back to the late 1800's. Early "word association" investigations by *Carl Jung* demonstrated measurable "arousal" or "*electro-dermal activity*" (EDA) related to the "emotional charge" maintained by an individual regarding key *words* and *concepts*. For our purposes, a *GSR-Meter* (or *EDA-Meter*) detects *emotional fluctuation*, measures *energetic fragmentation* and monitors changes in *Awareness* whenever a *Seeker* contacts "*charged*" terminals, *imprints* or *implants* on a particular channel.

Although design improvements (transistors, amplifiers, adjustable range &tc.) expanded its potential applications after the 1930's, the basic technology of *GSR-Meters* has remained stable and relatively unchanged since experimental research of *New Thought* movements emerging during the 1950's and 1960's.

Example of a "GSR-Meter"

One (or two) *"electrodes"* (*"sensors"* or *"probes"*) are held by, or attached to, the *Body* (*genetic-vehicle*). Early meters were little more than basic *"Ohmmeters"* lacking amplifiers and range control, making them difficult to use.

Volney G. Mathison developed the first *"Electro-Psychometer"* (the GSR *"E-Meter"*) with the intention of systematically applying the technology to *defragment* the *Human Condition*. [1950, Patent #2684670; *"Mathison Electrometer"* —using a single electrode held in one hand.]

Development and use of *GSR-Metering* for personal development followed along these systematic premises:

- *"Matter"* is the physical appearance of *"Energy"* (ZU)

as visible or detectable within the normative range of the *Human Condition*.

• *"Energy"* (ZU) is a "super-frequency" visible (or detectable) to *Humans* as *"matter"* or else manifest as the "stuff" of *"Mental Image Pictures."*

• *"Energy"* (ZU) may be directed by the (*Alpha*)-*Spirit* or *Self*; "raised," "lowered," "released" *&tc*.

• Improperly directed (or misdirected) *"Energy"* (ZU), "reduced flows" and/or "stuck flows," influence emotional states, personal illness and disease.

• An individual can modify *"Energy"* (ZU) flows, by selectively redirecting and applying *attention*, intentionally (*know-ingly*) duplicating "*Mental Image Patterns*" at a "conscious" level of *Awareness*.

• *"Psycho-Physical" Energy* (ZU) flows of the *Human Condition* register on, and may be relatively measured with, an *"Electro-Psychometer"* (GSR/EDA *"E-Meter"*).

> "Volney Mathison was a pioneer in the discovery that all fears, feelings and resentments—all thought and emotion—were electrical in their nature. He found through experiments with lie-detectors during the 1940's that when a person was reminded of certain past events, or when a change of mood was induced in him, the needle in the meter would jump erratically; the degree of jump was in proportion to the strength of unconscious reaction. In skilled hands, the meter could be used to locate particular mental content, the nature of that content, the location of that content in space and time, and the amount of force contained within it."
> —Peter Shepherd, <u>GSR Meter Course</u>
> *Tools for Transformation, 2001*

*An illustrated sample page from
Volney Mathison's "Super Visualization"*

Aside from "vintage" model *GSR Electro-Psychometers*, other *Biofeedback devices* that are appropriate (for our purposes) have appeared independently, with names such as: "Ability Meter" (*UK*); "Clarity Meter" (*US*); "Clearing Meter" (*generic term*); "Delta-1 Meter" (*Germany*); "Freedom-2 Meter" (*Russia*); "Mindwalker" (*UK*); and "Phoenix Meter"—just to name a few. More recent developments involve computer software. An *electrode* or *sensor* is connected to a "box" which transmits data displays to an existing device screen.

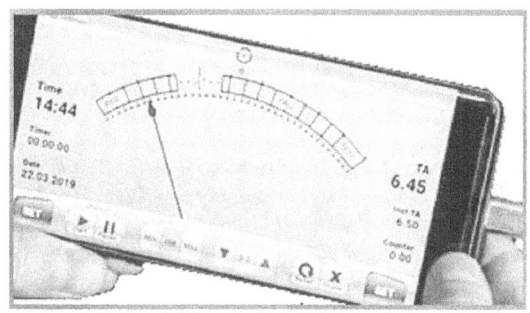

GSR technology displayed on a cell phone

Unless an individual plans to construct their own *GSR-Meter* (which is possible), the extent of "electrical" knowledge that a *Seeker* or *Pilot* needs to know is:

• Electrical *"current"* is electrical energy *"flow"*—meaning a *flow* (motion or action) of *electrons*, usually through a conductive wire; much like a *flow* of water moves through pipe or a hose.

• A "closed-loop" where *electrons* circulate (as a motion or activity) is called a *"circuit."*

• When referring to *"electrical resistance"* of a *circuit*, we quite literally mean: an *"energetic-mass"* (material) with an ability to *"restrict"* (slow down) *electron flow*.

- Larger or greater *electrical resistance* in a *circuit* indicates greater or denser *"mass" resisting free-flow* of *electrons* in that *circuit*.

> ### HISTORICAL FACT
> The basic electrical circuit used to measure an unknown (or variable) value of electrical resistance is called the *"Wheatstone bridge"*—named not for its original inventor (*Samuel Hunter Christie* in 1833), but for *Sir Charles Wheatstone*, an English scientist that improved and popularized its application and notoriety in 1843.

When a *Seeker* holds *electrodes* (*"sensors"*) of an *Electro-Psychometer* in their hands, they are part of a closed-circuit. A small amount of electrical current (usually no more than two volts) is passed through the *Body*, which now acts as one "leg" (or "side") of "resistance" in the circuit.

To determine the unknown value of *resistance* from the *Body*, a *"potentiometer"* (*"variable resistor"* and "range adjuster") is attached to the other "leg" ("side") and is controlled externally on the device by a rotating "knob" or "arm."

This "balancing arm" (or "baseline control") is manually rotated to a position where the "display-dial needle" is visibly at the "set" point, indicating a "balance point" is reached for the circuit.

While the "needle" is at the "set" point, the circuit is balanced: the "balancing arm" (or "baseline control") position on one "leg" or "side" of the "circuit bridge" indicates the *electrical resistance (*"ohms"*)* present across the surface of the skin on the other "leg" or "side" of the circuit.

> This is rather like using a "balancing scale" to determine the weight of something by adding a known amount (quantity/value/weight) to the other side.

All *GSR-Biofeedback devices* measure resistance, but may not display data in *ohms*. On Mathison's original models, arbitrary "number values" were assigned to the "balancing arm" for simplification, rather than use large "*ohms*" values. There was still a preassigned relationship between the two values. The following is only an example of this.

Balancing Arm	Resistance
1	500 Ω
2	5000 Ω
3	12,500 Ω
4	25,000 Ω
5	60,000 Ω
6	180,000 Ω

Standard *ohmmeters* feature display-dials covering such a large range that we don't see precise movements. *GSR-Meters* allow an individual to display a smaller portion (or range) of what the visible dial represents—and most have controls to increase or decrease amplification (sensitivity).

> "It is a remarkable fact that the real sources of one's anxiety may be so deeply hidden in one's subconscious that one will go about believing all sorts of other things are causing all the trouble, and erroneously blaming these other things which are *secon-*

> *dary effects*, not *causes*. Meanwhile, the *true cause* remains hidden, growing ever more powerful in its own *effects*."
>
> —V. Mathison, <u>Super-Visualization</u>
> Manual of Electropsychometry, 1956

> "When restimulated mental content is confronted, repression dissolves into *Awareness*. When not *confronted*, detachment may suffice, but if further involvement is enforced or encountered, then anxiety results."
>
> —Peter Shepherd, <u>GSR Meter Course</u>
> Tools for Transformation, 1994-2001

UNDERSTANDING GSR-BIOFEEDBACK FOR SPIRITUAL DEFRAGMENTATION

Prior to *Carl Jung's* incorporation of *GSR-Meters* for 'Word Association', the standard gauge of "psychoanalytics" primarily consisted of observing "*comm-lag*" (or *communication lag*); which is the amount of time it takes an individual to directly answer a question.

The intended purpose of *Systematic Processing* is to bring undesirable, implanted and artificial *programs*, *imprints* and *postulates* into clear view for a *Seeker* to analytically inspect "*As-It-Is*."

Suppressed *fragmentation*, *imprints* and *programming* are uncovered in layers—as some is taken off, more becomes accessible that previously might not even register on the *Meter*. This is elevation of *Actualized Awareness* in action and objectively on display to measure.

An individual that avoids "handling their stuff" runs the risk of having the *charge* restimulated by their environment in everyday life. Energy-flows encounter resistance from *mass*, just like damming up a stream of water. Hence, in most cases, the higher the resistance, the greater the *mass* encountered. Here we mean quite specifically and literally *"mental mass"* (or *"fields"*) surrounding certain 'ideas' and 'concepts'—or as *Carl Jung* was researching, associated with certain 'words' and 'memories'.

> As *energetically-entangled mental masses* are brought up to the "surface" for a *Seeker* to *confront*, the *resistance* may increase—or *"rise."* When the *mass* is actually *confronted As-It-Is* and disintegrated with the *Seeker's* "attention energy"—or else *"Actualized Awareness"*—then the *Meter* reads a *resistance* reduction, or *"fall."*

The device is not a substitute for understanding. A *Seeker* would already have to be familiar with vocabulary and concepts applied to a *process* or PCL. For example: a misunderstood word given in a *process* can cause false readings. Therefore, it is important to check each actual word used in a PCL prior to applying them, in order to be certain they do not already have a *"charge"* on them. This goes back to the original *Jungian* application of GSR for 'word association'.

A *GSR-Meter* is particularly useful when *Piloting* a *Seeker*. Although it does not indicate exactly *what* the *Seeker* is thinking about or confronting, it can indicate shifts in attention and *how* the *Seeker* is handling it.

Meters don't necessarily "read" the *Mind*—but they do register how the *Mind-System* is affecting the *Body* as it operates. For example: by observing the *Seeker* and *GSR-Meter*, a *Pilot* can determine when a *"hot-button"* is 'pressed' or *contacted* during *processing*—or when the *Seeker* is *withdrawing* (backing off) from the same.

There are indications for when the *Seeker* is experiencing *restimulation* of an *Imprint*—and also for when there is no longer a *"charge"* of entangled energy remaining on a particular circuit or channel.

The *Meters* are intended only as *tools* to assist *systematic processing* and should not be the ultimate focus. A *Pilot* is *processing* the *Seeker*; not the *Meter device* itself. It is also not a substitute for observing reactions and behaviors of a *Seeker*.

While it is true that excessively sweaty, cold or dry hands can affect the baseline read from the *electrodes* (and should be remedied before a *systematic session* begins), use of a *GSR-Meter* (as we describe and apply it) does not have anything to do with *"perspiration"*—which is what many skeptics and critics suggest. A *Human Body* does not sweat and "un-sweat" rapidly enough to provide the kind of instant *reactive reads* and changes we look for and observe during *systematic* use. By *reactive read*, we mean literally within an instant or second of a *Pilot* completing a statement, word or PCL. Anything more than three seconds and you are dealing with latent surface thought.

There are *Biofeedback* or *GSR-devices* on the market that do not possess the same features as the *Meters* described in this manual. Many of them should not really be called *"Meters."* They act more like "monitors," similar to a smoke detector. But those sold as "meditation trainers" or "stress-relaxation aids" likely resulted from a completely different type of experimental research than our own. That is not to say that this area does not require and deserve more research. A *Seeker* may find ways that they *can* be used.

In *processing sessions*, we are most interested in times when a *GSR-Meter* indicates a sudden *reduction* of *resistance*—or *"fall."* This denotes something that the *Seeker* is able to handle, *reach* for and is ready to *confront*; it denotes an increase in *Awareness* applied and a *willingness* to take *responsibility* for handling it. An *increase* or *"rise"* in *resistance* would indicate the opposite of this.

Of course, in order to have *"falls"* during a session there must be points when the *Meter* reads a rise—or that the Balance Point is at a relatively higher resistance. But, we are talking about *processing* each individual "item" or "terminal" (or an *imprinting incident* or event).

After *charge* on a particular area or item is indicated by a *"fall,"* the *needle* (*meter display*) will measure a *reduction* of *resistance* when the *Seeker* no longer resists directly handling/confronting it while *processing*.

A *Pilot* keeps an eye on the *Meter* to determine that a question or item is *"reading"* (causing a "change" on the *Meter*) before it is *systematically processed*. If it doesn't *"read"* then it isn't taken up in *processing* at that time.

Processing a *"charged"* terminal or incident continues so long as there is still a *"read"* (change) taking place. If there was no indicator (or *"read"*) to begin with, there would be no real way to gauge this; there would be no way to determine when a *Seeker* had effectively flattened that *wave-action* (or energetic *"ridge"*).

A *"ridge"* is perhaps one of the most *solid-state* "waveform patterns" encountered when an individual is working with *energies*. It is essentially an *"energetic-mass"* formed from two opposing *energy-wave flows*. In some ways, all physical *"matter"* could be considered a highly condensed and compacted energetic *"ridge."*

But rather than dissolving solid physical matter, we are concerned with *flattening* the "solidity" of *"collapsed wave-functions"* that form and collect as *"energetic-masses"* all around one's own *Personal Universe*. [See *Lesson-16* of the *Professional Course*.]

The "stuck" *Mental Image Pictures* and "reactive" *imprinting* are formed on-and-as such "ridges." And they have a tendency to build up into greater and greater *"masses"* when left improperly handled.

> When a *Seeker* is truly able and *willing*
> to handle, manage and/or *confront* the nature of their
> "stuff" *As-It-Is*, that increased *Awareness* is enough to
> "blow" the *fragmentation* apart.

A common experiment is to learn the "yes"/"no" *Meter*-reads and reactions by working with a list of questions (or generating them at the time) for which there is no mystery about the answers. For example: Are you sitting down? Are we presently inside/outside? Do you drive a car/have a license to drive a car? But nothing that digs to deep under the surface.

To get further practice and experience with what is taking place when using a *Meter* in session (and for handling *Ethics* or other *Integrity Checkups*), you can instruct a *Seeker* or partner to intentionally "lie" about an answer to a question that is otherwise obvious. For example: if they are sitting down—or if they are indoors—have them answer that they are not to each and see what and how things *"read."*

> "When [a mass or '*ridge*'] is restimulated by events or in session—if the material is too hard to experience or confront, it is repressed and there will not be an instantaneous response on the meter. The *ridge* will remain in restimulation but out of consciousness, until attention is directed to the item and it is confronted. This is a flight away from the *ridge*. If the client is able to view it, some of the suppressed emotional charge is released, causing a *fall* in resistance. This happens instantly. However, mental defenses may kick-in causing a backing off or resistance to the contents, because it may be hard to face. This stops the release of charge and the resistance may *rise*—still accessible but the client is fighting against it. A *rise*, then, relates to content that is being confronted, but is also fought against."
> —Peter Shepherd, <u>GSR Meter Course</u>
> *Tools for Transformation, 2001*

UNDERSTANDING GSR-METERS & HOW TO READ THEM

When working with a *GSR-Meter* for *systematic processing*, the most common term is *"read"*—like when you hear someone say, "that *reads*." More often than not it indicates a decrease in resistance or *"fall."*

There are also rare instances where the *Meter*, or more accurately, the observed *needle*, doesn't *read* anything at all for anything no matter what you do. The term *"stuck needle"* is often applied here, meaning that a *Seeker* is not offering their presence to the session. There is likely a break in *communication* (or a *"flow-factor"* as described in the *Professional Course*).

It is important to know whether or not a reaction is going to read, otherwise it gives an illusion that there is no "*charge*" on something, which may now be blown over—or *flown* over—when it should be handled. Operating a *session* in this way, when a *Seeker* is not providing presence, will actually reduce a *Seeker's* participation even further. The session, methods and *Pilot* lose credibility—even at "subconscious" levels; even when the *Seeker* is the one causing, allowing or validating the break in attention themselves.

So long as the sensitivity is kept constant then the *reads* on a *Meter* may be compared to other *reads*. For the "*falls*" you would be looking for the "largest" read or "*largest fall*" in relation to other *reads*. This is important when you are seeking to scout out a particular answer among variables.

For example: if you were to ask a *Seeker* which of their former jobs contributed to the most fragmentation, there may be some "*charge*" on more than one answer; therefore you are looking for the biggest reaction or *read* when each is named.

We often use the term "*resurfacing*" to denote bringing something into view that was hidden "beneath-the-surface." The quicker the response from a *Meter*, the closer something is to the "surface."

If something doesn't *read*, a *Pilot* should avoid focusing further attention on it. Of course, this does not mean that the *channel* is clear or there is no energetic *charge* held on the terminal in question—but it is not presently accessible or within the *Seeker's* reach or tolerance level to confront at that given time.

Without a *read*, there is no guarantee a *Pilot* can determine full erasure of that *fragmentation* or an *End Point*. This is what we mean about continuing a particular *process* or area of work so long as it is producing a change in *Awareness*; but not to a point of being *overrun*.

Using a *GSR-Meter* makes it a little easier for a *Pilot* to determine if an *End Point* is reached. It is critical to fully eliminate reactive *"charge"* from anything that either does *resurface*, or that can be made to *resurface*, so long as it is *reading* on the Meter. If a *Pilot* doesn't treat a *process* through to finality, then the *"Universe"* (*society, &tc.*) will most certainly keep *"running* it" and the *Seeker* will become increasingly withdrawn.

To establish a systematic standard for recording a *session*, we have established a chart for *Systemology* that applies to many *GSR-Meter* models used for spiritual defragmentation. On such models, the dial-display has a 90-degree range—showing a quarter of a circle. As illustrated, there is a *9-centimeter* arc of potential motion: *one centimeter* per *ten-degrees*.

In most cases, the area given to read the *"falls"* constitutes half of the *Meter*. It is the differences between reactions in this zone that are of primary interest for the session and its records.

Although not all practitioners with prior experience (using this type of technology) have the same interpretation for *reads*, using our chart offers the greatest stability or consistency in what we are looking for.

The Balance-Point or Set-Point provides a BASELINE reading and it reflects the basic state of a *Seeker* when at "rest" (presently in the session), without being aroused or directly *restimulated* by internal thought or the environment, *&tc.* A *read* is then taken when the needle moves off of, or out of, the small 15-degree region given for this. Sometimes a TINY TICK is *read* within this region; but if all session activity remains so close to the Balance-Point, it may be that the sensitivity is too low.

The answer to *"does it read?"* (hypothetical) could also be considered an answer to whatever "YES/NO" question you pose as a PCL. Therefore a *read* typically means "YES" or "there is something there."

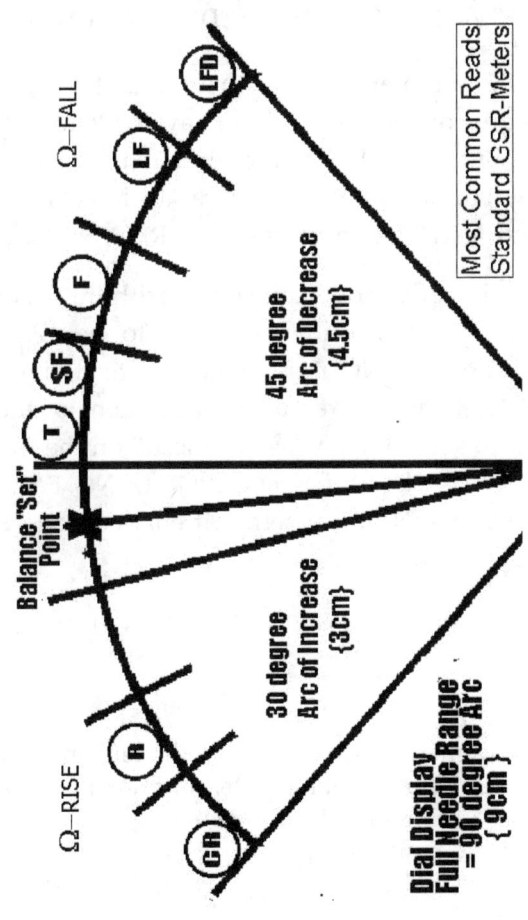

The Physical Universe is solidified by compacted matter that philosophically are "lies." When an individual is confronting (facing up to) the truth about something, they are practically disintegrating its effects on one's Personal Universe. Hence you get a reduced mass and reduced resistance ("fall"). Therefore, it is possible to get an increase-decrease fluctuation during a single process.

READING GSR-BIOFEEDBACK METERS

When a PCL or "item" results in a FALL, it means there is some degree of energetic "*charge*" available for a *Seeker* to *confront*. But then they could find while examining it, that they suddenly feel "resistive" to it, which literally adds "*resistance*" demonstrated by a RISE.

However, if a *Seeker* overcomes this withdrawal and continues to *confront* it, you will continue to see a FALL (usually a "LARGE/LONG FALL"/"LF") until it significantly "BALANCE DROPS" (requiring movement of the *Balancing-Arm* to keep the *needle* "balanced" on the *Meter dial-display*). Since this *read* is a LARGE/LONG FALL and a (BALANCE) DROP it is often written/recorded "LFD" or LFBD.

The basic *reads*, as they appear marked on our previous chart, are as follows:

(R) RISE (R)

Any movement of the needle on the left side of the "Set Point" (BA); no additional differentiation is made—unless it is a "Continuous Rise" (CR)—just the fact that the needle and resistance is *rising* (has *risen*). If it never did this you would not get any "*Balance-Arm* action" in *pro-*

cessing. An initial increase in resistance to a question means literally increased resistance *to* the question; it can *fall* once a *Seeker* permits themselves to confront it *As-It-Is*.

Since a *rise* generally indicates a *Seeker* does not want to confront what has been presented, it is best *not* to announce this *read* when it occurs. If pressed further in that direction the *Seeker* will break with *reality flow-factors* and *communication* and potentially go "out of session."

(CR) CONTINUOUS RISE (CR)

A large enough *rise* to the left side of the meter that requires the Balance-Arm to be adjusted to keep the needle within range of the dial-display. A question that immediately stops a "rising needle" is a change in characteristics and should be considered the same as a *Fall*.

Sessions where the *reads* do not seem to be coming as expected may require monitoring for any change in characteristics rather than other *reads*. So, if the needle is continuously *rising* but a question stops its motion—or it has been doing nothing but then decides to dance—this is a change in characteristics.

(BA)/(BP) BALANCE-ARM SET POINT (BA)/(BP)

The reading taken when the armature fixes the needle on the set point (or at least in the balanced range). If *Low* BA/BP—is below "2.0" (5000 *ohms*)—exceptionally decreased resistance possibly hyper-vigilant or overwhelmed; If *High* BA/BP—above "4.5" (35,000 *ohms*)—increased resistance is possibly withdrawal, dissociation and/or detachment.

If the BA/BP is *High* at the start of the session, the *Seeker's* attention is already directed on some "mass" elsewhere. You can start to free up these attention units by two-way communication with the *Seeker* about "where" their attention is.

"Do you have your attention on anything?" "Is there

anything you would like to tell me?" "Since your last session, is there anything that has happened?"

A Seeker is not trained in "solo-metering" for lower *processing-levels*. However, when combining two electrodes with a coupler—making certain the two do not touch—to hold in one hand, the BA/BP will be higher than standard (by a factor of as much as "0.5" higher) reads. Therefore what might be "2.1" (5500 *ohms*) when each electrode is held in its own hand, would then potentially be around "2.6" (9000 *ohms*) when *soloing* with one hand.

(X) NO/NULL READ (X)

As the name suggests, there is no read and the needle remains at rest at the "Set Point" (BA). "No charge" or an answer of "no" should be distinguishable from a "stuck needle" based on characteristics of meter reads throughout the *session* up to this point or from a proper *session* setup that guarantees the *Seeker* is participating or has presence in *session*.

(T) TICK/TINY READ (T)

A rapid *fall* of less than a few millimeters to the right of the "Set Point" (BA); as the name suggests, it barely counts as read. It may or may not even leave the "Balanced Range." If you get a small "trace read" from a question, trying varying the wording. If the same small "tick" or "tiny read" is all that occurs after three inquiries, move on.

(SF) SMALL/SHORT FALL (SF)

Up to one centimeter (or ½ an inch) *fall* to the right side of the "Set Point" (BA). Any amount of *fall* is still a *fall*; if you are still getting a *read* after several runs or exhausted question/answer, the *Seeker* still "hasn't told all" or else you are dealing with a "past life" or an area they do not "consciously know about."

If a decent *read* occurs when the *Seeker* hasn't said anything, inquire about it. "What was that there?" "What did you just think of there?" "Did you have a thought there?"

(F) FALL (F)

One to two centimeters (½ inch to one inch) *fall* to the right side of the "Set Point" (BA). Any length of *fall* is a standard *read* or "Yes" answer to your question; for some techniques (*processes*) the largest/longest *fall*-read is the answer.

(LF) LARGE/LONG FALL (LF)

Two to six centimeters (1 to 3 inches) *fall* to the right side of the "Set Point" (BA). Among several possible *reads*, the largest/longest *read* or *fall* is the answer.

(LFD/LFBD) LARGE/LONG FALL BALANCE DROP

A large enough *fall* to the right side of the meter that requires the Balance- Arm to be adjusted to keep the needle within range of the dial-display. A massive discharge of this caliber accompanies the *Seeker* having confronted (faced-up-to) or seeing (knowingly duplicating creation of) something *As-It-Is*, thereby duplicating and eradicating what and where something is by consciously placing one's own there—seeing it for what *It Is* on one's own volition.

> "If the [*Seeker*] knew about the subconscious reactive contents of the mind, they wouldn't be subconscious or reactive. But the *GSR-Meter* responds to the reactive emotional charge. Hence, you don't follow up something unless it gives a read. You don't let the [*Seeker's*] analytical (cognitive) mind control the session or give it free reign to talk about anything it likes. It is a [*Pilot's*] responsibility to control the session. The [*Pilot*] has more control over the [*Seeker's*] case, since the [*Seeker*] is influenced by the case."
>
> —Peter Shepherd, <u>GSR Meter Course</u>
> *Tools for Transformation, 2001*

APPLYING GSR-METERS TO SYSTEMATIC PROCESSING

This course supplement has provided a tremendous amount of basic fundamentals regarding history, purposes and usage of *GSR-Biofeedback Meters*. Volney Mathison's own publication (*"Super-Visualization"*) includes a basic *"session script"* that offers examples of what might be expected when applying *GSR-Meters* to methods similar to our own presentation of *systematic processing* in previous lessons.

Use of a *Meter* does not in itself solve the matter of getting the *Seeker* to participate *presence* in *sessions*, with attention fully on *processing*; there are no substitutes for skillfully *Piloting* a *Seeker*—it must be learned and practiced. This includes actual certainty on handling a *Meter* when it is applied to *processing*; and this is best gained only by experience.

Having the *Seeker* "squeeze the cans" (and then release) is a popular way of setting/adjusting the *sensitivity* before a *session* really begins. Intentional "squeezes" should only produce a one-inch *fall*. The device can be adjusted for this. It also shows the difference between an actual *"read"* versus simply adding *"pressure."*

Once a *process* has begun, it is best if the *sensitivity* does not have to be readjusted. When you are rapidly comparing relative "lengths" of various *falls*, the *sensitivity* must remain constant. There are some instances (especially in *Ethics Processing* for *Personal Integrity*) when you really want to see if a question is getting a solid *read* or not. You can always raise the *sensitivity* for that particular PCL, but make sure to return it to where it was afterward.

If everything that you are asking or saying is getting large reads, you may need to turn the *sensitivity* down. A simple determinant of basic stress levels can be observed at the beginning of a *session* to check this. Simply ask: *"How are you going to feel about my asking you a lot of personal questions?"*

Of course, we are not really concerned about a *Seeker's* answer, so much as what kind of *read* is observed. If there is a strong *read* in response to this, it is likely that the *Seeker* has experienced uncomfortable interrogation in the past, either from a family member or some other source. It is helpful if communication can be used between the *Pilot* and *Seeker* to quiet these *reads* before proceeding. This occurs simply by identifying the underlying source of the *turbulence*.

If a *Seeker's* attention is not directed precisely on the session and PCL, there is no way to determine what the *reads* on a *Meter* actually pertain to. Having the *Seeker* acknowledge the *Pilot*—a reality on the fact that the *Pilot* is the *Pilot*—is quite critical for the *Pilot* being able to get (and keep) the *Seeker in-session*.

There is at least one key reason why this is sometimes difficult—and this can be checked with the *Meter* prior to a true session start. *Pilot* asks: *"Do I remind you in some way of a person you have known whom you feared or disliked?"*

If there is no *read* on that, or if there is only a *tiny tick*, consider rephrasing the PCL slightly: *"Is there anything about me that is similar to some person that bothered or injured you in the past?"* If any of these types of questions indicates a YES, then *defragment* that line using basic communication regarding the underlying issue. Resolving things like this is, of course, critical for success; but it also directly facilitates getting the *Seeker* to participate with *presence* in the *session*.

> "A sharp prolonged meter surge on *'How do you feel about your name?'* indicates one of two things: the (*Seeker*) is using a false, an assumed, or an altered name—or—more commonly, the (*Seeker*) dislikes their name for some specific reason which they can readily clarify. A disliked name has some unpleasant or silly connotation or association. Sometimes a name is changed to forget a hated parent, a past mate, or the like. Meter surges on such situations are all significant and should be discussed until tension on them subsides. Laughter, yawns and sighs will cause major needle surges, owing to flash metabolic effects, and may, in general, be disregarded. Do not permit the (*Seeker*) to tap on the electrode with finger or thumb. Minor needle surges may merely indicate mental activity. Major surges indicate areas of pain or tension."
> —Volney Mathison, <u>Super-Visualization</u>
> Manual of Electropsychometry, 1956

As a chiropractor, Mathison's initial interests for using an *"Electro-psychometer"* pertained to the physiological body long before concepts of *spiritual defragmentation* became paramount. Therefore, in his manual—prior to the *Test Questionnaire* (given hereafter)—he describes a progressive *'Deep Meditation' technique* that is otherwise very similar to *'Energetic Body Scanning'*.

For example: a *Pilot* gives the PCL: "Toes, left foot, relax." [Or, alternatively to "relax": "Let go" or "Let go of the tension."]

The *Seeker* would then silently deliver the PCL/message

to the *Body* (*genetic vehicle*) and report back with "Okay" after having done so. The *Pilot* closes that communication cycle with an acknowledgment ("*Thank You*") and begins the next cycle: "*Now, ankle, left foot, relax.*" And onward in this fashion, treating each portion of the *Body*.

If at any point the *Pilot* sees a "sharp needle surge" on the *Meter* in relation to a certain part of the body, nothing is said, but a notation is made. Once a list of all *Body* areas is completed, the *Pilot* returns to those which were indicated and if the unrest still persists, additional *attention* is given to them with the PCL: "*Be at ease.*"

Here is the original *Test Questionnaire* that appears in Mathison's *Electropsychometry Manual* (from 1956). Strong *reads* or "surges" (as he calls them) should be reduced with *processing* and *communication* (techniques described in the *Professional Course*). As an "assessment," this is really meant to "open a case" and not necessarily "solve" every aspect of a *Seeker's* life. It allows a *Pilot* to get a general idea of where some significant trouble-spots are. An attempt should be made, however, to reduce the "*charge*" on anything found to give major *reads* before continuing on with other standard *processing-levels*.

MATHISON'S QUESTIONNAIRE

1. How do you feel about your name?

2. What is your occupation? How do you feel about it?

3. How do you feel about your mother? About your father?

4. What sort of person do you fear? Hate?

5. Mention one of the worst things that has happened to you.

6. What do you think of a person that commits suicide? [*A heavy surge may indicate a suicide risk or that they a Seeker has lost someone close this way.*]

7. Have you ever been in a hospital?

8. Have you ever been injured in an accident?

9. Whom did you hate or fear most when you were a child?

10. Mention some things you are very anxious about or that you feel should not occur. Mention some things you would fight or struggle against to keep them from happening.

11. Who loves you?

12. Who used to love you, but no longer does?

13. Can you think of a time when you wished someone would love you?

14. Do you feel remorse, regret or blame over the way you have treated some person? Mother? Father? Wife? Husband? *&tc.*

15. If you were writing a novel and you had to depict some injurious thing happening to a baby or a child, what would have this thing be?

16. Have you ever been struck or severely beaten?

17. How do you think women feel about you?

18. How do you think men feel about you?

19. How do you think children feel about you?

20. Have you ever been through an unhappy love experience?

21. Do you love your wife/husband? [*This is asked without the mate present.*]

22. How do you think your wife/husband feels about you?

23. Have you ever been attacked or severely shocked sexually? [*It may not be advisable to explore this content directly; particularly if the Seeker and Pilot are unfamiliar to each other and/or of different genders.*]

24. Are you presently satisfied with your sexual activities?

25. Have you ever had a bitter quarrel with a man? Woman? Mention actual incidents.

26. What do you think about the use of contraceptives? Abortions?

27. What do you think about illegitimate children?

28. What do you think of a woman who is frigid? Or a man who is impotent?

29. What do you think of a sexual sadist? Masochist?

30. Have you ever been jeered at, made fun of, or painfully rejected?

31. What things do you keep doing that you wish you didn't do?

32. What changes do you wish to make in yourself?

33. Mention three goals or ambitions that you have wished to achieve—and which you have achieved.

34. Mention three goals or ambitions that you have wished to achieve—and which you have not achieved.

ADVANCED APPLICATIONS &
THE PROFESSIONAL COURSE

In *Traditional Piloting*, if a *Seeker* slows or stalls on the *Pathway*, it is up to the *Pilot* to determine why. Of course, really it is only the *Seeker*, themselves, that knows—even if they don't think that it is the reason why. But, it is still a *Pilot's* responsibility to discover it for all concerned, and often this involves probing various areas directly (often with assistance of an *GSR-biofeedback device*). In *Solo-Piloting*, a *Seeker* must discover, *identify* and *confront* the underlying fundamental *breaks, upsets,* and *fragmentation*, themselves, with or without assistance of a *GSR-Meter*.

Starting with *Systemology Level-5* (*Lesson-11* of the *Professional Course*), a *Seeker* begins dealing more with "*things*" (*terminals* and *forms*) and "*incidents*" that are not directly encountered (or typically visible) from within the normative "confines" or "limitations" of the *Human Condition*. Although they continue to affect our experience of *Beta-Existence*, they "perturb" and "impinge" upon our *reality* as an "unseen source" of various creations, personal reactivity and manifestations in our *Personal Universe*.

Biofeedback devices may be used to detect when *fragmented charge* in certain "unseen areas" is present. So, what we are speaking of is not entirely "undetectable," just not always *knowingly* sensed, especially if it is presently "active" or "*restimulated.*"

Some basic techniques for "*defragmenting implants*" (for *advanced processing*) are given in the *Professional Course*. For *Level-5*, without a meter, the basic procedure is:

A. *"Spot (or Imagine) an implant-item (or command-item in the listed sequence)."*

B. *"Confront it until it ceases to have any effect."*

The easiest way for a *Seeker* to accomplish this is to alternately:

A. *"Spot the implanted command-item."*

B. *"Spot something in the room."*

"Command-Items" are/were not *implanted* in "English" (or any language of Human speech). Therefore, the best we can do for *processing* is to *"approximate"* their meaning (*get a sense* for their original *intention*) when each *"command-item"* is *"Spotted."*

When a *GSR-Meter* is applied to this practice, then *"Step-B"* is technically replaced with *"Spotting the Meter display for reads."* Note that these *reads* occur rather quickly; it is best to maintain a view of both the *list* and the *Meter*.

A *Seeker* *"Spots"* the *"item"* on a certain list and then immediately checks the *Meter* for a *"read."* This continues, alternating *attention* between the *"item"* and the *Meter* until no *"charge"* is *reading*. A *Seeker* *"runs"* this *process* on each *"item"* given on the list. This same method applies to *processing-out* other *considerations*.

APPENDIX REFERENCE MATERIAL

FOUNDATIONS OF SYSTEMOLOGY

Mardukite Zuism is a precursor to *Systemology*. It concerns an intensive archaeological study into the *Arcane Tablets* of Ancient Mesopotamia. Such tablet writings were once used to systematize an understanding of all cosmic knowledge—and they include the Babylonian *Epic of Creation*.

The *Epic of Creation* describes *ALL* ("ANKI") as separated into two *existences*: "AN" and "KI"—literally "heaven" and "earth"—which is to say *"spiritual"* ("AN") and *"physical"* ("KI"). Exterior to, and beyond, the *"potential everythingness"* of all *spiritual* existence and *physical* existence is only an Infinity of Nothingness ("ABZU").

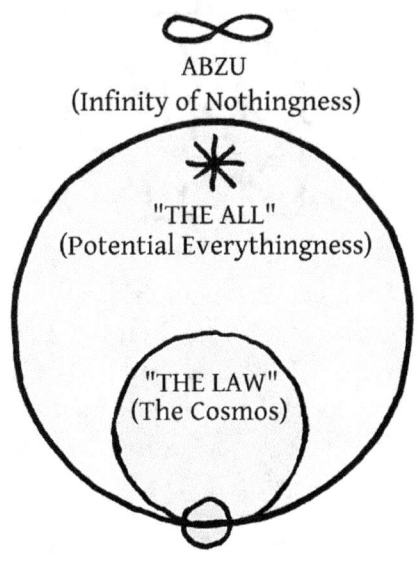

In *Systemology*, we refer to the same two separate states of existence as *"Alpha"* (*spiritual*) and *"Beta"* (*physical*). They are connected only by *"Spiritual Life Awareness"* or *"ZU"*—a term we have retained in *Systemology* (and for which *Mardukite Zuism* is named). Therefore, we have *"spiritual systems"* and *"physical systems"* connected by *"ZU."*

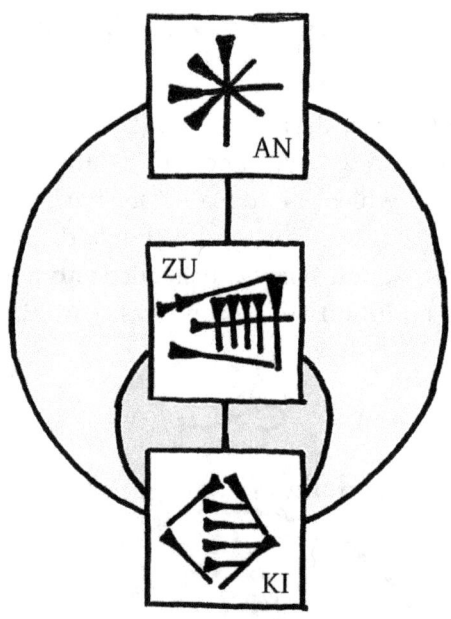

The *"Alpha" Universe*—of *"metaphysical"* or *"spiritual"* energy-matter—is not dependent on the *"Beta" Universe* to exist. The two exist independent of one another, except for a single channel or conduit maintaining a connection, which *is* the *Awareness* (the *Spiritual Life-Energy* or *"ZU"*) of an *"Alpha-Spirit."*

"ZU" originates from an *"Alpha"* (*spiritual*) state, separate and distinct from the conditions of *"Beta"* existence that

we experience as the *Physical Universe*. "ZU" is *Awareness* —the *Life-Force* or *Thought-Power* that "acts" or "impinges" on an "organism" in *Beta-Existence*.

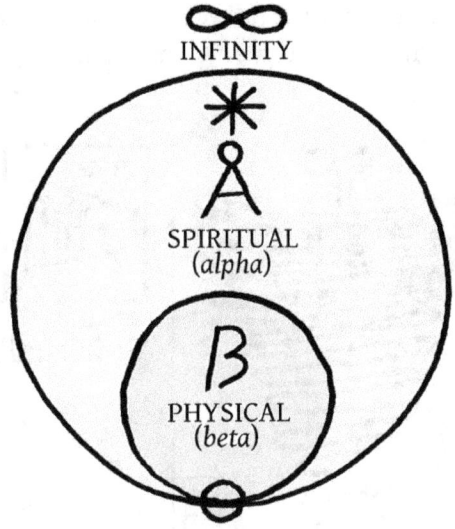

For example: the "intention" to read this book, or "command" a body to turn a page—those specific components are not actually a part of *this* existence. They are manifestations of a *Spiritual Awareness* (*Alpha*) acting upon an "organic body" (*Beta*). The *"Alpha-Spirit"* is the actual "Eternal" *Self*, which perceives and engages with *Beta-Existence* (*e.g.*, "Life on Earth") by using a "temporary" organic body or *"genetic vehicle."*

The *Alpha-Spirit* engages a *"ZU-Line"*—a spiritual "lifeline" of *Attention* and *Awareness* ("ZU") energy—to an "organic body" or *genetic-vehicle* in order to directly experience a *"physical"* Beta-Existence.

We use the term *"Self-Honesty"* in *Systemology* to describe the original native *"Alpha"* state of true *Self-Directed* "Be-

ingness" and crystal clear "*Knowingness.*" *Self-Honesty* is the most basic "personality" or true expression of *Self* (*Alpha-Spirit*) as "*I-AM*"—a *Self-Determined* state that is *free* of artificial attachments, automatic reaction-response mechanisms, or enforced (*other-determined*) "*reality-agreements*" concerning the Human Condition.

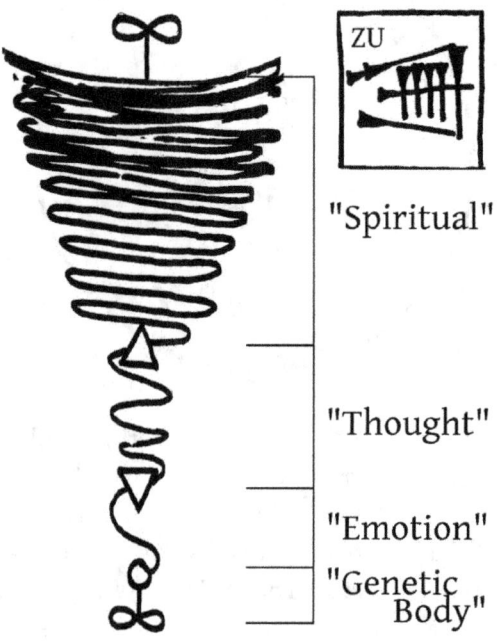

Applying philosophic routes and systematic methods of *Systemology* in order to return *Awareness* of *Self* to its true "*Source*" is referred to as "*The Pathway.*" Its structure is based on archaic "models" from the "Ancient Near East" (*Mesopotamia, &tc.*) and elsewhere—such as the "*Chakras,*" the Babylonian "*Ladder of Lights*" (*Star-Gates*), and several versions of "*Kabbalah.*"

THE STANDARD MODEL OF SYSTEMOLOGY

– – *ALPHA* – –

8. "INFINITY"
7. The Alpha-Spirit (*Home Universe*)
6. Alpha-Thought (*Creation and Imagination*)
5. Will-Intention (*Alpha Equivalent of Effort*)

– – *BETA* – –

4. "MCC" (*Command of a Mind*)
3. Analytical (*Associative Knowledge*)
2. "RCC" (*Control of Biochemical Activity*)
1. Emotional (*Stored Data of Loss and Pain*)
0. Effort (*Solidity of the Physical Universe*)

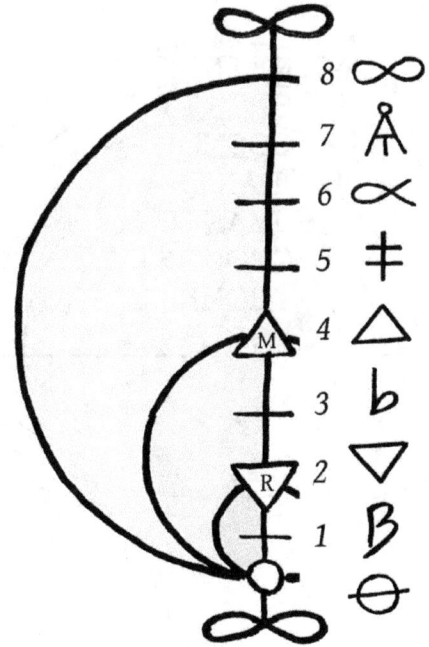

THE SPHERES OF EXISTENCE MODEL

– – *METAHUMAN* – –

8. "INFINITY"
7. Alpha (*All Life in Spiritual Existence*)
6. Universe (*All Life in Beta-Existence*)
5. Planet (*All Life on Earth, Trees, Animals...*)

– – *HUMAN* – –

4. Species (*All Humans*)
3. Societies (*Groups, Organizations*)
2. Home (*Domestic, Family, Children*)
1. Self (*The Individual*)

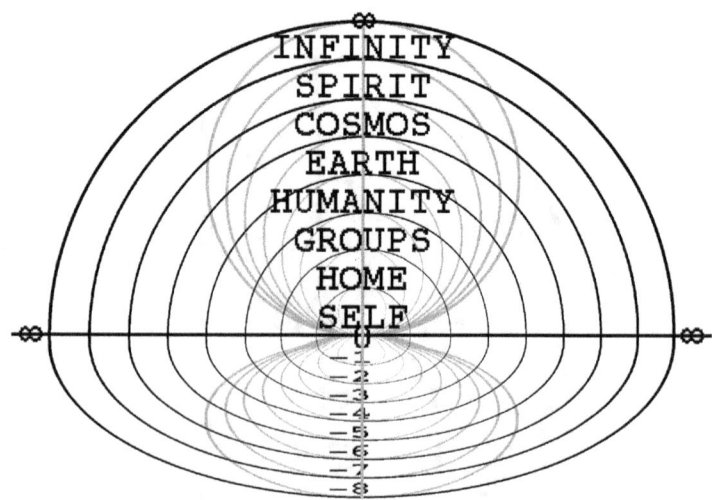

BASIC SYSTEMOLOGY GLOSSARY

A-for-A (one-to-one) : an expression meaning that what we say, write, represent, think or symbolize is a direct and perfect reflection or duplication of the actual aspect or thing—that "A" is for, means and is equivalent to "A" and not "a" or "q" or "!"; in the relay of communication, the message or particle is sent and perfectly duplicated in form and meaning when received.

actualization : to make actual, not just potential; to bring into full solid Reality; to realize fully in *Awareness* as a "thing."

affinity : the apparent and energetic *relationship* between substances or bodies; the degree of *attraction* or repulsion between things based on natural forces; the *similitude* of frequencies or waveforms; the degree of *interconnection* between systems.

agreement (reality) : unanimity of opinion of what is "thought" to be known; an accepted arrangement of how things are; things we consider as "real" or as an "is" of "reality"; a consensus of what is real as made by standard-issue (common) participants; what an individual contributes to or accepts as "real"; in *Systemology*, a synonym for "*reality.*"

alpha : the first, primary, basic, superior or beginning of some form; in *Systemology*, referring to the state of existence operating on spiritual archetypes and postulates, will and intention "exterior" to the low-level condensation and solidity of energy and matter as the 'physical universe'.

alpha-spirit : a "spiritual" *Life*-form; the "true" *Self* or I-AM; the *individual*; the spiritual (*alpha*) *Self* that is animating the (*beta*) physical body or "*genetic vehicle*" using a continuous *Lifeline* of spiritual ("*ZU*") energy; an individual spiritual (*alpha*) entity possessing no physical mass or measurable waveform (motion) in the Physical Universe as itself, so it animates the (*beta*) physical body or "*genetic vehicle*" as a catalyst to experience *Self*-determined causality in effect within the *Physical Universe*; a singular unit or point of *Spiritual Awareness* that is *Aware* that it is *Aware*.

alpha thought : the highest spiritual *Self-determination* over creation and existence exercised by an Alpha-Spirit; the Alpha range of pure *Creative Ability* based on direct postulates and considerations of *Beingness*; spiritual qualities comparable to "thought" but originating in Alpha-existence (at "6.0") independently superior to a *beta-anchored* Mind-System, although an Alpha-Spirit may use Will ("5.0") to carry the intentions of a postulate or consideration ("6.0") to the Master Control Center ("4.0").

apparent : visibly exposed to sight; evident rather than actual, as presumed by Observation; readily perceived, especially by the senses.

archetype : a "first form" or ideal conceptual model of some aspect; the ultimate prototype of a form on which all other conceptions are based.

ascension : actualized *Awareness* elevated to the point of true "spiritual existence" exterior to *beta existence*. An "Ascended Master" is one who has returned to an incarnation on Earth as an inherently *Enlightened One*, demonstrable in their actions—they have the ability to *Self-direct* the "Spirit" as *Self* and maintain consciousness beyond this existence as a personal identity continuum with the same *Self-directed* control and communication of Will-Intention that is exercised, actualized and developed deliberately during one's present incarnation.

assessment : an analysis or synthesis of collected information, usually about a person or group, in relation to an *assessment scale*.

associative knowledge : significance or meaning of a facet or aspect assigned to (or considered to have) a direct relationship with another facet; to connect or relate ideas or facets of existence with one another; a reactive-response image, emotion or conception that is suggested by (or directly accompanies) something other than itself; in traditional systems logic, an equivalency of significance or meaning between facets or sets that are grouped together, such as in *(a + b) + c = a + (b + c)*; in Systemology, erroneous associative knowledge is assignment of the same value to all facets or parts considered as related (even when they are not actually so), such as in $a = a, b = a, c = a$ and so forth without distinction.

attention : active use of *Awareness* toward a specific aspect or thing; the act of "attending" with the presence of *Self*; a direction of focus or concentration of *Awareness* along a particular channel or conduit or toward a particular terminal node or communication termination point; the Self-directed concentration of personal energy as a combination of observation, thought-waves and consideration; focused application of *Self-Directed Awareness*.

awareness : the highest sense of-and-as Self in knowing and being as I-AM (the *Alpha-Spirit*); the extent of beingness directed as a POV experienced by Self as knowingness.

axiom : a fundamental truism of a knowledge system, esp. *logic*; all *maxims* are also *axioms*; knowledge statements that require no proof because their truth is self-evident; an established law or systematic principle used as a *premise* on which to base greater conclusions of truth.

beta (awareness) : all consciousness activity ("*Awareness*") in the "Physical Universe" (KI) or else *beta-existence*; *Awareness* within the range of the *genetic-body*, including material thoughts, emotional responses and physical motors; personal *Awareness* of physical energy and physical matter moving through physical space and experienced as "time"; the *Awareness* held by *Self* that is restricted to a physical organic *Lifeform* or "*genetic vehicle*" in which it experiences causality in the *Physical Universe*.

beta (existence) : all manifestation in the "Physical Universe" (KI); the "Physical" state of existence consisting of vibrations of physical energy and physical matter moving through physical space and experienced as "time"; the conditions of *Awareness* for the *Alpha-spirit* (*Self*) as a physical organic *Lifeform* or "*genetic vehicle*" in which it experiences causality in the *Physical Universe*.

beta-defragmentation : toward a state of *Self-Honesty* in regards to handling experience of the "Physical Universe" (*beta-existence*); an applied spiritual philosophy (or technology) of Self-Actualization originally described in the text "*Crystal Clear*" (*Liber-2B*), building upon theories from "*Systemology: The Original Thesis*."

catalyst : something that causes action between two systems or aspects, but which itself is unaffected as a variable of this energy communication; a medium or intermediary channel.

chakra : an archaic Sanskrit term for "wheel" or "spinning circle" used in *Eastern* wisdom traditions, spiritual systems and mysticism; a concept retained in Systemology to indicate etheric concentrations of energy into wheel-mechanisms that process *ZU* energy at specific frequencies along the *ZU-line*, of which the *Human Condition* is reportedly attached *seven* at various degrees as connected to the Gate symbolism.

channel : a specific stream, course, current, direction or route; to form or cut a groove or ridge or otherwise guide along a specific course; a direct path; an artificial aqueduct created to connect two water bodies or water or make travel possible.

charge : to fill or furnish with a quality; to supply with energy; to lay a command upon; in *Systemology*—to imbue with intention; to overspread with emotion; application of *Self-directed (WILL)* "intention" toward an emotional manifestation in beta-existence; personal energy stores and significances entwined as fragmentation in mental images, reactive-response encoding and intellectual (and/or) programmed beliefs; in traditional mysticism, to intentionally fix an energetic resonance to meet some degree, or to bring a specific concentration of energy that is transferred to a focal point, such as an object or space.

circuit : a circular path or loop; a closed-path within a system that allows a flow; a pattern or action or wave movement that follows a specific route or potential path only; in *Systemology*, "*communication processing*" pertaining to a specific flow of energy or information along a channel; *see* also "*feedback loop.*"

communication : successful transmission of information, data, energy (&tc.) along a message line, with a reception of feedback; an energetic flow of intention to cause an effect (or duplication) at a distance; the personal energy moved or acted upon by will or else 'selective directed attention'; the 'messenger action' used to transmit and receive energy across a medium; also relay of energy, a message or signal—or even locating a personal POV (viewpoint) for the Self—along the *ZU-line*.

compulsion : a failure to be responsible for the dynamics of control—starting, stopping or altering—on a particular channel of communication and/or regarding a particular terminal in existence; an energetic flow with the appearance of being 'stuck' on the action it is already doing or by the control of some automatic mechanism.

concept : a high-frequency thought-wave representing an "idea" which persists because it is not restricted to a unique space-time; an abstract or tangible "idea" formed in the "Mind" or *imagined* as a means of understanding, usually including associated "Mental Images"; a seemingly timeless collective thought-theme (or subject) that entangles together facets of many events or incidents, not just a single significant one.

condense (condensation) : the transition of vapor to liquid; denoting a change in state to a more substantial or solid condition; leading to a more compact or solid form.

condition : an apparent or existing state; circumstances, situations and variable dynamics affecting the order and function of a system; a series of interconnected requirements, barriers and allowances that must be met; in "contemporary language," bringing a thing toward a specific, desired or intentional new state (such as in "conditioning"), though to minimize confusion about the word "condition" in our literature, *Systemology* treats "contemporary conditioning" concepts as imprinting, encoding and programming.

conflict : the opposition of two forces of similar magnitude along the same channel or competing for the same terminal; the inability to duplicate another POV; a thought, intention or communication that is met with an opposing counter-thought or counter-intention that generates an energetic cluster.

confront : to come around in front of; to be in the presence of; to stand in front of, or in the face of; to meet "face-to-face" or "face-up-to"; additionally, in *Systemology*, to fully tolerate or acceptably withstand an encounter with a particular manifestation or encounter.

consciousness : the energetic flow of *Awareness*; the Principle System of *Awareness* that is spiritual in nature, which demonstrates potential interaction with all degrees of the Physical Universe; the *Beingness* component of our existence in *Spirit*; the Principle System of *Awareness* as *Spirit* that directs action in the Mind-System.

consideration : careful analytical reflection of all aspects; deliberation; determining the significance of a "thing" in relation to similarity or dissimilarity to other "things"; evaluation of facts and importance of certain facts; thorough examination of all aspects related to, or important for, making a decision; the analysis of consequences and estimation of significance when making decisions; in *Systemology*, the postulate or Alpha-Thought that defines the state of beingness for what something "*is.*"

continuity : being a continuous whole; a complete whole or "total round of"; the balance of the equation ["–120" + "120" = "0" *&tc.*]; an apparent unbroken interconnected coherent whole; also, as applied to Universes in *Systemology*, the lowest base consideration of space-time or commonly shared level of energy-matter apparent in an existence, or else the lowest degree of solidity or condensation whereby all mass that exists is identifiable or communicable with all other mass that exists; represented as "0" on the *Standard Model* for the Physical Universe (*beta-existence*), a level of existence that is below Human emotion, comparable to the solidity of "rocks" and "walls" and "inert bodies."

continuum : a continuous enduring uninterrupted sequence or condition; observing all gradients on a *spectrum*; measuring quantitative variation with gradual transition on a spectrum without demonstrating discontinuity or separate parts.

control (general) : the ability to start, change or start some action or flow of energy; the capacity to originate, change or stop some mode of human behavior by some implication, physical or psychological means to ensure compliance (voluntarily or involuntarily).

control (systems) : communication relayed from an operative center or organizational cluster, which incites new activity elsewhere in a system (or along the *ZU-line*)

defragmentation : the *reparation* of wholeness; collecting all dispersed parts to reform an original whole; a process of removing "*fragmentation*" in data or knowledge to provide a clear understanding; applying techniques and processes that promote a *holistic* interconnected *alpha* state, favoring observational *Awareness* of continuity in all spiritual and physical systems; in *Systemology*, a "*Seeker*" achieving an actualized state of basic "*Self-Honest Awareness*" is said to be *beta-defragmented*, where as *Alpha-defragmentation* is the rehabilitation of the *creative ability*, managing the *Spiritual Timeline* and the POV of *Self* as Alpha-Spirit (I-AM); see also "*Beta-defragmentation*."

degree : a physical or conceptual *unit* (or point) defining the variation present relative to a *scale* above and below it; any stage or extent to which something *is* in relation to other possible positions within a *set* of "*parameters*"; a point within a specific range or spectrum; in *Systemology*, a *Seeker's* potential energy variations or fluctuations in thought, emotional reaction and physical perception are all treated as "*degrees*."

dramatization / dramatize : a vivid display or performance as if rehearsed for a "play" (on stage); a *'circuit'* recording *'imprinted'* in the past and, once restimulated by a facet of the environment, the individual "replays" it as through reacting to it in the present (and identifying that reality as present reality); acts, actions and observable behaviors that demonstrate identification with a particular character type, "phase" or personality program; a motivated sequence-chain, implant series or imprinted cycle of actions—usually irrational or counter-survival—repeated by an individual as it had previously happened to them; a reoccurring or reactively triggered out-flow, communication or action that indicates an individual "occupying" a particular *'Point-of-View'* (*POV*)—typically fixed to a specific (past) identification (identity) that is space-time locatable (meaning a point where significant *Attenergy*—enough to compulsively create and maintain a POV—is "stuck" or "hung up" on the *BackTrack*).

dynamic (systems) : a principle or fixed system which demonstrates its *'variations'* in activity (or output) only in constant relation to variables or fluctuation of interrelated systems; a standard principle, function, process or system that exhibits *'variations'* and change simultaneously with all connected systems; each *'Sphere of Existence'* is a dynamic system, systematically affecting (supporting) and affected (supported) by other *'Spheres'* (which are also dynamic systems).

emotional encoding : the readable substance/material (data) of *'imprints'*; associations of sensory experience with an *imprint*; perceptions of our environment that receive an *emotional charge*, which form or reinforce facets of an *imprint*; perceptions recorded and stored as an *imprint* within the "emotional range" of energetic manifestation; the formation of an energetic store or charge on a channel that fixes emotional responses as a mechanistic automation, which is carried on in an individual's *Spiritual Timeline* (or personal continuum of existence).

encompassing : to form a circle around, surround or envelop around.

end point : the moment when the goal of a process has been achieved and to continue on with it will be detrimental to the gains; the finality of a process when the *Seeker* has achieved their optimum state from the current cycle (whether or not they run through it again at a later date with a different level of *Awareness* or knowledge base doesn't change the fact that it has flattened the standing wave

enforcement : the act of compelling or putting (effort) into force; to compel or impose obedience by force; to impress strongly with applications of stress to demand agreement or validation; the lowest-level of direct control by physical effort or threat of punishment; a low-level method of control in the absence of true communication.

evaluate : to determine, assign or fix a set value, amount or meaning.

existence : the *state* or fact of *apparent manifestation*; the resulting combination of the Principles of Manifestation: consciousness, motion and substance; continued *survival*; that which independently exists; the *'Prime Directive'* and sole purpose of all manifestation or Reality; the highest common intended motivation driving any "*Thing*" or *Life*.

exterior : outside of; on the outside; in *Systemology*, we mean specifically the POV of *Self* that is *'outside of'* the *Human Condition,* free of the physical and mental trappings of the Physical Universe; a metahuman range of consideration; see also '*Zu-Vision*'.

external : a force coming from outside; information received from outside sources; in *Systemology*, the objective *'Physical Universe'* existence, or *beta-existence*, that the Physical Body or *genetic vehicle* is essentially *anchored* to for its considerations of locational space-time as a dimension or POV.

facets : an aspect, an apparent phase; one of many faces of something; a cut surface on a gem or crystal; in *Systemology*—a single perception or aspect of a memory or "*Imprint*"; any one of many ways in which a memory is recorded; perceptions associated with a painful emotional (sensation) experience and "*imprinted*" onto a metaphoric lens through which to view future similar experiences; other secondary terminals that are associated with a particular terminal, painful event or experience of loss, and which may exhibit the same encoded significance as the activating event.

faculties : abilities of the mind (individual) inherent or developed.

feedback loop : a complete and continuous circuit flow of energy or information directed as an output from a source to a target which is altered and return back to the source as an input; in *General Systemology*—the continuous process where outputs of a system are routed back as inputs to complete a circuit or loop, which may be closed or connected to other systems/circuits; in *Systemology*—the continuous process where directed *Life* energy and *Awareness* is sent back to *Self* as experience, understanding and memory to complete an energetic circuit as a loop.

flow : movement across (or through) a channel (or conduit); a direction of active energetic motion typically distinguished as either an *in-flow*, *out-flow* or *cross-flow*.

fragmentation : breaking into parts and scattering the pieces; the *fractioning* of wholeness or the *fracture* of a holistic interconnected *alpha* state, favoring observational *Awareness* of perceived connectivity between parts; *discontinuity*; separation of a totality into parts; in *Systemology*, a person outside a state of *Self-Honesty* is said to be *fragmented*.

game : a strategic situation where a "player's" power of choice is employed or affected; a parameter or condition defined by purposes, freedoms and barriers (rules).

general systemology ("systematology") : a methodology of analysis and evaluation regarding the systems—their design and function; organizing systems of interrelated information-processing in order to perform a given function or pattern of functions.

genetic-vehicle : a physical *Life*-form; the physical (*beta*) body that is animated/controlled by the (*Alpha*) *Spirit* using a continuous *Lifeline* (ZU); a physical (*beta*) organic receptacle and catalyst for the (*Alpha*) *Self* to operate "causes" and experience "effects" within the *Physical Universe*.

gradient : a degree of partitioned ascent or descent along some scale, elevation or incline; "higher" and "lower" values in relation to one another.

hold-back : withheld communications (esp. actions) such as "*Hold-Outs*"; intentional (or automatic) withdrawal (as opposed to reach); Self-restraint (which may eventually be enforced or automated); not reaching, acting or expressing, when one should be; an ability that is now restrained (on automatic) due to inability to withhold it on Self-determinism alone.

hold-outs : in photography, the numerous snapshots/pictures withheld from the final display or professional presentation of the event; withheld communications; in Utilitarian Systemology—energetic withdrawal and communication breaks with a "*terminal*" and its *Sphere of Existence* as a result of a "*Harmful-Act*"; unspoken or undiscovered (hidden, covert) actions that an individual withholds communications of, fearing punishment or endangerment of *Self-preservation* (*First Sphere*); the act of hiding (or keeping hidden) the truth of a "*Harmful-Act*"; a refusal to communicate with a *Pilot*; also "*Hold-Back*."

holistic : the examination of interconnected systems as encompassing something greater than the *sum* of their "parts."

Human Condition : a standard default state of Human experience that is generally accepted to be the extent of its potential identity (*beingness*)—currently treated as *Homo Sapiens Sapiens,* but which is scheduled for replacement by *Homo Novus*.

identification : the association of *identity* to a thing; a label or fixed data-set associated to what a thing is; association "equals" a thing, the "equals" being key; an equality of all things in a group, for example, an "apple" identified with all other "apples"; the reduction of "I-AM"-*Self* from a *Spiritual Beingness* to an "identity" of some form.

identity : the collection of energy and matter—including memory—across a "*Spiritual Timeline*" that we consider as "I" of *Self*, but the "I" is an individual and not an identification with anything other than *Self* as *Alpha-Spirit*.

imagination : the ability to create *mental imagery* in one's Personal Universe at will and change or alter it as desired; the ability to create, change and dissolve mental images on command or as an act of will; to create a mental image or have associated imagery displayed (or "conjured") in the mind that may or may not be treated as real (or memory recall) and may or may not accurately duplicate objective reality; to employ *Creative Abilities* of the Spirit that are independent of reality agreements with beta-existence.

imprint : to strongly impress, stamp, mark (or outline) onto a softer 'impressible' substance; to mark with pressure onto a surface; in *Systemology*, the term is used to indicate permanent Reality impressions marked by frequencies, energies or interactions experienced during periods of emotional distress, pain, unconsciousness, loss, enforcement, or something antagonistic to physical (personal) survival, all of which are are stored with other reactive response-mechanisms at lower-levels of *Awareness* as opposed to the active memory database and proactive processing center of the Mind; an experiential "memory-set" that may later resurface—be triggered or stimulated artificially—as Reality, of which similar responses will be engaged automatically; holographic-like imagery "stamped" onto consciousness as composed of energetic *facets* tied to the "snap-shot" of an experience.

imprinting incident : the first or original event instance communicated and *emotionally encoded* onto an individual's "*Spiritual Timeline*" (recorded memory from all lifetimes), which formed a permanent impression that is later used to mechanistically treat future contact on that channel; the first or original occurrence of some particular *facet* or mental image related to a certain type of *encoded response*, such as pain and discomfort, losses and victimization, and even the acts that we have taken against others along the Spiritual Timeline of our existence that caused them to also be *Imprinted*.

inhibited : withheld, held-back, discouraged or repressed from some state.

"in phase" : see "*phase alignment.*"

intention : the directed application of Will; to intend (have "in Mind") or signify (give "significance" to) for or toward a particular purpose; in *Systemology* (from the *Standard Model*)—the spiritual activity at WILL (5.0) directed by an *Alpha Spirit* (7.0); the application of WILL as "Cause" from a higher order of Alpha Thought and consideration (6.0), which then may continue to relay communications as an "effect" in the universe.

interior : inside of; on the inside; in *Systemology*, we mean specifically the POV of *Self* that is fixed to the *'internal' Human Condition,* including the *Reactive Control Center* (RCC) and Mind-System or *Master Control Center* (MCC); within *beta-existence*.

internal : a force coming from inside; information received from inside sources; in *Systemology*, the objective *'Physical Universe'* experience of *beta-existence* that is associated with the Physical Body or *genetic vehicle* and its POV regarding sensation and perception; from inside the body; within the body.

invalidate : decrease the level or degree or *agreement* as Reality.

knowledge : clear personal processing of informed understanding; information (data) that is actualized as effectively workable understanding; a demonstrable understanding on which we may 'set' our *Awareness*—or literally a "know-ledge."

Master-Control-Center (MCC) : a perfect computing device to the extent of the information received from "lower levels" of sensory experience/perception; the proactive communication system of the "*Mind*"; a relay point of active *Awareness* along the Identity's *ZU-line*, which is responsible for maintaining basic *Self-Honest Clarity* of *Knowingness* as a *seat of consciousness* between the *Alpha-Spirit* and the secondary "*Reactive Control Center*" of a *Lifeform* in *beta existence*; the Mind-center for an *Alpha-Spirit* to actualize cause in the *beta existence*; the analytical *Self-Determined* Mind-center of an *Alpha-Spirit used* to project *Will* toward the genetic body; the point of contact between *Spiritual Systems* and the *beta existence*; presumably the "*Third Eye*" of a being connected directly to the *I-AM-Self*, which is responsible for *determining* Reality at any time; in *Systemology*, this is plotted at (4.0) on the continuity model of the *ZU-line*.

mental image : a subjectively experienced "picture" created and imagined into being by the Alpha-Spirit (or at lower levels, one of its automated mechanisms) that includes all perceptible *facets* of totally immersive scene, which may be forms originated by an individual, or a "facsimile-copy" ("snap-shot") of something seen or encountered; a duplication of wave-forms in one's Personal Universe as a "picture" that mirror an "external" Universe experience, such as an *Imprint*.

methodology : a complete system of applications, methods, principles and rules to compose a *'systematic'* paradigm as a "whole"—esp. a field of philosophy or science.

misappropriated : put into use incorrectly; to apply ineffectively or as unintended by design or definition.

objective : concerning the "external world" and attempts to observe Reality independent of personal "subjective" factors.

one-to-one : see "*A-for-A.*"

optimum : the most favorable or ideal conditions for the best result; the greatest degree of result under specific conditions.

organic : as related to a physically living organism or carbon-based life form; energy-matter condensed into form as a focus or POV of Spiritual Life Energy (*ZU*) as it pertains to beta-existence of *this* Physical Universe (*KI*).

paradigm : an all-encompassing *standard* by which to view the world and *communicate* Reality; a standard model of reality-systems used by the Mind to filter, organize and interpret experience of Reality.

parameters : a defined range of possible variables within a model, spectrum or continuum; the extent of communicable reach capable within a system or across a distance; the defined or imposed limitations placed on a system or the functions within a system; the extent to which a Life or "thing" can *be*, *do* or *know* along any channel within the confines of a specific system or spectrum of existence.

patterns (probability patterns) : observation of cycles and tendencies to predict a causal relationship or determine the actual condition or flow of dynamic energy using a holistic systemology to understand Life, Reality and Existence as opposed to isolating or excluding perceived parts as being mutually separate from other perceived parts.

perception : internalized processing of data received by the *senses*; to become *Aware of* via the senses.

personality (program) : the total composite picture an individual "identifies" themselves with; the accumulated sum of material and mental mass by which an individual experiences as their timeline; a "beta-personality" is mainly attached to the identity of a particular physical body and the total sum of its own genetic memory in combination with the data stores and pictures maintained by the Alpha Spirit; a "true personality" is the Alpha Spirit as Self completely defragmented of all erroneous limitations and barriers to consideration, belief, manifestation and intention.

phase (identification) : in *Systemology*, a pattern of personality or identity that is assumed as the POV from *Self*; personal identification with artificial "personality packages"; an individual assuming or taking characteristics of another individual (often unknowingly as a response-mechanisms); also "*phase alignment.*"

phase alignment or "*in phase*" : to be in synch or mutually synchronized, in step or aligned properly with something else in order to increase the total strength value; in *Systemology*, alignment or adjustment of *Awareness* with a particular identity, space or time; perfect *defragmentation* would mean being "in phase" as *Self* fully conscious and Aware as an Alpha-Spirit *in* present *space* and *time*, free of synthetic personalities.

physics : regarding data obtained by a material science of observable motions, forces and bodies, including their apparent interaction, in the Physical Universe (specific to this *beta-existence*).

physiology : a material science of observable biological functions and mechanics of living organisms, including codification and study of identifiable parts and apparent systematic processes (specific to agreed upon makeup of the *genetic vehicle* for this *beta-existence*).

pilot : a professional steersman responsible for healthy functional operation of a ship toward a specific destination; in *Systemology*, an intensive trained individual qualified to specially apply *Systemology Processing* to assist other *Seekers* on the *Pathway*.

point-of-view (POV) : a point to view from; an opinion or attitude as expressed from a specific identity-phase; a specific standpoint or vantage-point; a definitive manner of consideration specific to an individual phase or identity; a place or position affording a specific view or vantage; circumstances and programming of an individual that is conducive to a particular response, consideration or belief-set (paradigm); a position (consideration) or place (location) that provides a specific view or perspective (subjective) on experience (of the objective).

postulate : to put forward as truth; to suggest or assume an existence *to be*; to state or affirm the existence of particular conditions; to provide a basis of reasoning and belief; a basic theory accepted as fact; in *Systemology*, "Alpha-Thought"—the top-most decisions or considerations made by the Alpha-Spirit regarding the "*is-ness*" (what things "are") about energy-matter and space-time.

potentiality : the total "sum" (collective amount) of "latent" (dormant—present but not apparent) capable or possible realizations; used to describe a state or condition of what has not yet manifested, but which can be influenced and predicted based on observed patterns and, if referring to beta-existence, Cosmic Law.

presence : the quality of some thing (energy/matter) being "present" in space-time; personal orientation of *Self* as an *Awareness* (*POV*) located in present space-time (environment) and communicating with extant energy-matter.

Prime Directive : a "spiritual" implant program that installs purposes and goals into the personal experience of a Universe, esp. any *Beta-Existence* (whether a 'Games Universe' or a 'Prison Universe'); intellectually treated as the "Universal Imperative" in some schools of moral philosophy; comparable to "Universal Law" or "Cosmic Ordering."

"process-out" : to reduce *emotional encoding* of an *imprint* to zero; to dissolve a *wave-form* or *thought-formed* "solid" such as a "*belief*"; to completely run a *process* to its end, thereby *flattening* any previous *waves* of *fragmentation* that are obstructing the *clear channel* of *Self-Awareness*; also referred to as "processing-out"; to discharge all previously held emotionally encoded imprinting or erroneous programming and beliefs that otherwise fix the free flow (wave) to a particular pattern, solid or concrete "*is*" form.

processing command line (PCL) or **command line** : a directed input; a specific command using highly selective language for *Systemology Processing*; a predetermined directive statement (cause) intended to focus concentrated attention (effect).

processing, systematic : the inner-workings or "through-put" result of systems; in *Systemology*, a methodology of applied spiritual technology used toward personal Self-Actualization; methods of selective directed attention, communicated language and associative imagery that targets an increase in personal control of the human condition.

reactive control center (RCC) : the secondary (reactive) communication system of the "*Mind*"; a relay point of *Awareness* along the Identity's *ZU-line*, which is responsible for engaging basic motors, biochemical processes and any *programmed automated responses* of a living *beta* organism; the reactive Mind-Center of a living organism relaying communications of *Awareness* between causal experience of *Physical Systems* and the "*Master Control Center*"; it presumably stores all emotional encoded imprints as fragmentation of "chakra" frequencies of *ZU* (within the range of the "*psychological/emotive systems*" of a being), which it may *react* to as Reality at any time; in *Systemology*, this is plotted at (2.0) on the continuity model of the *ZU-line*.

reality : see "*agreement.*"

realization : the clear perception of an understanding; a consideration or understanding on what is "actual"; to make "real" or give "reality" to so as to grant a property of "beingness" or "being as it is"; the state or instance of coming to an *Awareness*; in *Systemology*, "gnosis" or true knowledge achieved during *systematic processing*; achievement of a new (or "higher") cognition, true knowledge or perception of Self; a consideration of reality or assignment of meaning.

relative : an apparent point, state or condition treated as distinct from others.

responsibility : the *ability* to *respond*; the extent of mobilizing *power* and *understanding* an individual maintains as *Awareness* to enact *change*; the proactive ability to *Self-direct* and make decisions independent of an outside authority.

resurface : to return to (or bring up to) the "surface" of that which has previously been submerged; in *Systemology*—relating specifically to processes where a *Seeker* recalls blocked energy stored covertly as emotional "*imprints*" (by the RCC) so that it may be effectively defragmented from the "*ZU-line*" (by the MCC).

Seeker : an individual on the *Pathway to Self-Honesty*; a practitioner of *Mardukite Systemology* or *Systemology Processing* that is working toward *Spiritual Ascension*.

Self-actualization : bringing the full potential of the Human spirit into Reality; expressing full capabilities and creativeness of the *Alpha-Spirit*.

Self-determinism : the freedom to act, clear of external control or influence; the personal control of Will to direct intention.

Self-honesty : the basic or original *alpha* state of *being* and *knowing*; clear and present total *Awareness* of-and-as *Self*, in its most basic and true proactive expression of itself as *Spirit* or *I-AM*—free of artificial attachments, perceptive filters and other emotionally-reactive or mentally-conditioned programming imposed on the human condition by the systematized physical world; the ability to experience existence without judgment.

sensation : an external stimulus received by internal sense organs (receptors/sensors); sense impressions.

slate : a hard thin flat surface material used for writing on; a chalk-board, which is a large version of the original wood-framed writing slate, named for the rock-type it was made from.

spectrum : a broad range or array as a continuous series or sequence; defined parts along a singular continuum; in physics, a gradient arrangement of visible colored bands diffracted in order of their respective wavelengths, such as when passing *White Light* through a *prism*.

Spheres of Existence (dynamic systems) : a series of *eight* concentric circles, rings or spheres (each larger than the former) that is overlaid onto the Standard Model of Beta-Existence to demonstrate the dynamic systems of existence extending out from the POV of Self (often as a "body") at the *First Sphere*; these are given in the basic eightfold systems as: *Self*, *Home/Family*, *Groups*,

Humanity, Life on Earth, Physical Universe, Spiritual Universe and *Infinity-Divinity.*

spiritual timeline : a continuous stream of moment-to-moment *Mental Images* (or a record of experiences) that defines the "past" of a spiritual being (or *Alpha-Spirit*) and which includes impressions (*imprints, &tc.*) form all life-incarnations and significant spiritual events the being has encountered; in Systemology, also "*backtrack.*"

standard issue : equally dispensed to all without consideration.

Standard Model, The (systemology) : in *Systemology*—our existential and cosmological *standard model* or cabbalistic model; a "*monistic continuity model*" demonstrating *total system* interconnectivity "above" and "below" observation of any apparent *parameters*; the original presentation of the *ZU-line*, represented as a singular vertical (y-axis) waveform in space across dimensional levels or Universes (*Spheres of Existence*) without charting any specific movement across a dimensional time-graph x-axis; The Standard Model of Systemology represents the basic workable synthesis of common denominators in models explored throughout Grade-I and Grade-II material.

static : characterized by a fixed or stationary condition; having no apparent change, movement or fluctuation.

succumb : to give way, or give in to, a relatively stronger superior force.

system : from the Greek, "to set together"; to set or arrange things or data together so as to form an orderly understanding of a "whole"; also a *'method'* or *'methodology'* as an orderly standard of use or application of such data arranged together.

systematization : to arrange into systems; to systematize or make systematic.

terminal (node) : a point, end or mass on a line; a point or connection for closing an electric circuit, such as a post on a battery terminating at each end of its own systematic function; any end point or 'termination' on a line; a point of connectivity with other points; in systems, any point which may be treated as a contact point of interaction; anything that may be distinguished as an 'is' and is therefore a 'termination point' of a system or along a flow-line which may interact with other related systems it shares a line with; a point of interaction with other points.

thought-form : apparent *manifestation* or existential *realization* of *Thought-waves* as "solids" even when only apparent in Reality-agreements of the Observer; the treatment of *Thought-waves* as permanent *imprints* obscuring *Self-Honest Clarity* of *Awareness* when reinforced by emotional experience as actualized "thought-formed solids" ("*beliefs*") in the Mind; energetic patterns that "surround" the individual.

thought-habit : reoccurring modes of thought or repeated "self-talk"; essentially "self-hypnosis" resulting in a certain state.

thought-wave or **wave-form** : a proactive *Self-directed action* or reactive-response *action* of *consciousness*; the *process* of *thinking* as demonstrated in *wave-form*; the *activity* of *Awareness* within the range of *thought vibrations/frequencies* on the existential *Life-continuum* or *ZU-line*.

threshold : a doorway, gate or entrance point; the degree to which something is to produce an effect within a certain state or condition; the point in which a condition changes from one to the next.

tier : a series of rows or levels, one stacked immediately before or atop another.

time : observation of cycles in action; motion of a particle, energy or wave across space; intervals of action related to other intervals of action as observed in Awareness; a measurable wave-length or frequency in comparison to a static state; the consideration of variations in space.

timeline : plotting out history in a linear (line) model to indicate instances (experiences) or demonstrate changes in state (space) as measured over time; a singular conception of continuation of observed time as marked by event-intervals and changes in energy and matter across space.

turbulence : a quality or state of distortion or disturbance that creates irregularity of a flow or pattern; the quality or state of aberration on a line (such as ragged edges) or the emotional "turbulent feelings" attached to a particular flow or terminal node; a violent, haphazard or disharmonious commotion (such as in the ebb of gusts and lulls of wind action).

understanding : a clear 'A-for-A' duplication of a communication as 'knowledge', which may be comprehended and retained with its significance assigned in relation to other 'knowledge' treated as a 'significant understanding'; the "grade" or "level" that a knowledge base is collected and the manner in which the data is organized and evaluated.

validation : reinforcement of agreements or considerations as "real."

viewpoint : see "*point-of-view*" *(POV)*.

will *or* **WILL** (5.0) : in *Systemology* (from the *Standard Model*), the Alpha-ability at "5.0" of a Spiritual Being (*Alpha Spirit*) at "7.0" to apply *intention* as "Cause" from consideration or Alpha-Thought at "6.0" that is superior to "beta-thoughts" that only manifest as reactive "effects" below "4.0" and *interior* to the *Human Condition*.

willingness : the state of conscious Self-determined ability and interest (directed attention) to *Be*, *Do* or *Have*; a Self-determined consideration to reach, face up to (*confront*) or manage some "mass" or energy; the extent to which an individual considers themselves able to participate, act or communicate along some line, to put attention or intention on the line, or to produce (create) an effect.

ZU : the ancient Sumerian cuneiform sign for the archaic verb —"*to know,*" "*knowingness*" or "*awareness*"; in *Mardukite Zuism and Systemology*, the active energy/matter of the "Spiritual Universe" (AN) experienced as a *Lifeforce* or *consciousness* that imbues living forms extant in the "Physical Universe" (KI); "*Spiritual Life Energy*"; energy demonstrated by the WILL of an actualized *Alpha-Spirit* in the "Spiritual Universe" (AN), which impinges its *Awareness* into the Physical Universe (KI), animating/controlling *Life* for its experience of *beta-existence* along an individual Alpha-Spirit's personal *Identity-continuum*, called a *ZU-line*.

***Zu*-Line** : a theoretical construct in *Mardukite Zuism and Systemology* demonstrating *Spiritual Life Energy* (*ZU*) as a personal individual "continuum" of Awareness interacting with all Spheres of Existence on the Standard Model of Systemology; a spectrum of potential variations and interactions of a monistic continuum or singular *Spiritual Life Energy (ZU)* demonstrated on the Standard Model; an energetic channel of potential POV and "locations" of Beingness, demonstrated in early Systemology materials as an individual Alpha-Spirit's personal *Identity-continuum*, potentially connecting *Awareness (ZU)* of *Self* with "*Infinity*" simultaneous with all points considered in existence; a symbolic demonstration of the "*Life-line*" on which *Awareness (ZU)* extends from the direction of the "Spiritual Universe" (AN) in its true original *alpha state* through an entire possible range of activity resulting in its *beta state* and control of a *genetic-entity* occupying the *Physical Universe (KI)*.

Zu-Vision : the true and basic (*Alpha*) Point-of-View (perspective, POV) maintained by *Self* as *Alpha-Spirit* outside boundaries or considerations of the *Human Condition* "Mind-Systems" and *exterior* to beta-existence reality agreements with the Physical Universe; a POV of Self *as* "a unit of Spiritual Awareness" that exists independent of a "body" and entrapment in a *Human Condition*; "spirit vision" in its truest sense.

WOULD

YOU

LIKE

TO

KNOW

MORE

? ? ?

AVAILABLE FROM THE **JOSHUA FREE** PUBLISHING IMPRINT

SYSTEMOLOGY

FUNDAMENTALS OF SYSTEMOLOGY

A New Thought for the 21st Century

The Official
New Standard Systemology
Basic Course

ALL *Six Lessons* in one
Collector's Edition hardcover
or *paperback workbook*

All *six* lesson-booklets of the first official
Basic Course on Mardukite Systemology
are combined together in *one volume* as
"Fundamentals of Systemology."

Also available individually.

"Being More Than Human"

"Realities in Agreement"

"Windows To Experience"

"Ancient Systemology"

"A History of Systemology"

"Systemology Processing"

AVAILABLE FROM THE **JOSHUA FREE** PUBLISHING IMPRINT

SYSTEMOLOGY

THE PATHWAY TO ASCENSION

Spiritual Clearing

The Official
New Standard Systemology
Professional Course

ALL *Sixteen Lessons* in *two*
Collector's Edition hardcovers
or *one paperback workbook*

All *sixteen* lesson-booklets of the *New Standard Professional Course* on Mardukite Systemology are combined together for the *first time* as **"The Pathway to Ascension."**

Also available individually.

"Increasing Awareness"
"Thought & Emotion"
"Clear Communication"
"Handling Humanity"
"Free Your Spirit"
"Escaping Spirit-Traps"
...and more!

AVAILABLE FROM THE **JOSHUA FREE** PUBLISHING IMPRINT

SYSTEMOLOGY

KEYS TO THE KINGDOM

Spiritual Clearing (Levels 7 and 8)

The Official
New Standard Systemology
Advanced Training Course

ALL *Eight Manuals* in *two Collector's Edition hardcovers* or *one paperback workbook*

All *eight* A.T. lesson-manuals of the *New Standard Advanced Training Course* on Mardukite Systemology are combined together for the *first time* as **"Keys to the Kingdom."**

Also available individually.

"The Secret of Universes"

"Games, Goals and Purposes"

"The Jewel of Knowledge"

"Implanted Universes"

"Entities and Fragments"

"Spiritual Perception"

...and more!

AVAILABLE FROM THE **JOSHUA FREE** PUBLISHING IMPRINT

SYSTEMOLOGY
The Pathway to Self-Honesty

THE ORIGINAL UNDERGROUND INTRODUCTIONS

SYSTEMOLOGY
The Original Thesis of Mardukite New Thuoght
by Joshua Free
(*Mardukite Systemology Liber-S-1X*)

The very first underground discourses released to the "New Thought" division of the Mardukite Research Organization privately over a decade ago and providing the inspiration for a rapid futurist spiritual technology called *"Mardukite Systemology."*

THE POWER OF ZU
Applying Mardukite Zuism & Systemology to Everyday Life
by Joshua Free
Foreword by Reed Penn
(*Mardukite Systemology Liber-S-1Z*)

A unique introductory course on Mardukite Zuism & Systemology, including transcripts from a 3-day lecture series given by Joshua Free in December 2019 specifically to launch the Mardukite Academy of Systemology & the Founding Church of Mardukite Zuism *just in time for the 2020's.*

Seekers and students of the *Basic Course* and *Professional Course* will also be interested in the *Systemology Core Research Volumes*. These eight volumes are a complete chronological record of the *Mardukite New Thought* developments from the *Systemology Society*, published in 2019 through 2023.

Our *Systemology Core Research Archive* begins with the first professional publication released when the *Mardukite Systemology Society* emerged into public view from the underground in 2019: *"The Tablets of Destiny Revelation."*

The Tablets of Destiny Revelation:
*How Long-Lost Anunnaki Wisdom
Can Change the Fate of Humanity*

Crystal Clear: *Handbook for Seekers*

Metahuman Destinations (*2 volumes*)

Imaginomicon:
Approaching Gateways to Higher Universes

Way of the Wizard: *Utilitarian Systemology*

Systemology-180: *Fast-Track to Ascension*

Systemology Backtrack:
Reclaiming Spiritual Power & Past-Life Memory

AVAILABLE FROM THE **JOSHUA FREE** PUBLISHING IMPRINT

IN A WORLD FULL OF "TENS" BE AN
ELEVEN

THE METAPHYSICS OF STRANGER THINGS

TELEKINESIS, TELEPATHY SYSTEMOLOGY

by Joshua Free

Mardukite Systemology Liber-011

Experimental exploratory edition

Discover the metaphysical truth about the Universe—and maybe even yourself—as you explore what lies beneath the epic saga, *Stranger Things*. You're invited to a world where fantasy, science fiction and horror unite—and the ideas behind games like *Dungeons and Dragons* become a reality.

Uncover a world of secret "mind control" projects, just like those at *Hawkins National Laboratory*. Decades of psychedelic experiments among other developmental programs for psychic powers, remote viewing, telekinesis (psychokinesis, PK) and more are revealed. Get an inside look at the operations of a modern real-life underground organization pursuing the truth about rehabilitating spiritual abilities for an actual "metahuman" evolution on planet Earth.

Premiere edition available in paperback and hardcover!

AVAILABLE FROM THE **JOSHUA FREE** PUBLISHING IMPRINT

Commemorating the 15th Anniversary!

NECRONOMICON
THE COMPLETE ANUNNAKI BIBLE
(*Deluxe Edition Hardcover*)
collected works by Joshua Free

The ultimate masterpiece of Mesopotamian magic, spirituality and history, providing a complete collection—a grand symphony—of the most ancient writings on the planet. The oldest Sumerian and Babylonian records reveal detailed accounts of cosmic history in the Universe and on Earth, the development of human civilization and descriptions of a world order that is unparalleled today.

All of this information has been used, since ancient times, to maintain spiritual and physical control of humanity and its systems. It has proved to be the predecessor and foundation of all global scripture-based religious and mystical traditions thereafter. These are the raw materials, unearthed from the underground, which have shaped humanity's beliefs, traditions and existence for thousands of years—right from the heart of the Ancient Near East: Sumer, Babylon and even Egypt...

∞

PUBLISHED BY THE **JOSHUA FREE** IMPRINT REPRESENTING

**The Founding Church of Mardukite Zuism
& Mardukite Academy of Systemology**

mardukite.com

www.ingramcontent.com/pod-product-compliance
Lightning Source LLC
Chambersburg PA
CBHW071143060526
44107CB00131B/184